The Spur Master Guide to Ski Touring

Also by Rob Hunter:

Spur Venture Guide Series

Cross Country Skiing
Parallel Skiing
Walking
The Camping and Backpacking Cook Book
Jogging
Chart & Compass

and with Terry Brown:

Basic Skiing
Knots, Bends & Hitches
Sailing
Camping
Snorkelling
Outdoor First Aid
Weather Lore
Map & Compass
Survival & Rescue
Winter Camping
also
The Outdoor Companion (Constable)

The Spur Master Guide to
Ski Touring

ROB HUNTER

SPURBOOKS LIMITED

Published by
Spurbooks Limited
6 Parade Court,
Bourne End,
Buckinghamshire

ISBN 0 904978 41 9

Designed and Produced by
Mechanick Exercises, London

Printed in Great Britain by
Galbraith King & Co. Ltd, London

Contents

Acknowledgements

I would like to thank the following for advice, suggestions, hints and tips in the writing of this book. John Poole of the Y.H.A. XC-Ski Dept.; Patrick Goyet of Toulouse, France; Bill Evans of W3 Adventure Inc., Quebec; The Ski Schools of Voss, Norway and Villard de Lans, Vercors, France, and La Chaise Dieu, Auvergne in the Massif Central; Cameron McNeish, Aviemore; John Traynor; Terry Brown; John Rae of Rossignol and, as always, Estelle Huxley.

1979   ROB HUNTER

Publisher's Introduction

ABOUT THIS SERIES

This book, a Master Guide to Ski Touring, follows the publication of a successful series of outdoor handbooks for *beginners*. Master Guides are *not* for beginners. They are for those people who have had one or two years experience in some chosen outdoor activity, and now wish to develop it, or they are concerned with outdoor activities which, by their very nature are not for *beginners*. Master Guides will initially cover such subjects as Ski Mountaineering, Snow Camping, Advanced Rock Climbing, Long Distance Walking, Expeditions, Outdoor Skills, and, the subject of this book, Cross Country (XC) Ski Touring. Further titles will follow.

ABOUT THIS BOOK

Ski Touring is a growing activity in all the mountain and snowfield areas of the world. This springs from the mammoth growth in cross country skiing over the last few years, itself a reaction from the crowds on the downhill slopes. Touring offers even more opportunities to flee from the masses and therefore enjoys increasing popularity.

Moreover, ski touring attracts a vast audience from the summer wanderers, backpackers and walkers. The object of this book is to tell all such people, who already have many of the necessary skills (whether skiers or not) how to start ski touring, how to plan their trips and develop touring expertise how to travel about the winter hills in safety, and have a good time in the process. The diagrams are drawn to illustrate points in the text and should be studied closely.

ABOUT THE AUTHOR

Rob Hunter is an outdoor writer, traveller, and publisher; author or co-author of over twenty books on outdoor skills or activities, and a regular contributor to outdoor magazines. He has ski toured in Europe and North America, in Norway, the Pyrénées, Scotland, the Appalachians, the Alps and the Canadian Rockies, for over twenty years.

1 · What is Ski-Touring?

Getting away from it all is increasingly hard to do. The crowds and the endless pressures are everywhere, even in the winter hills. One way to avoid them there is to take up ski touring and leave the bustle behind and the aim of this book is to show you how.

The name, ski-touring, is subject to various definitions, and on its own can be an all-embracing term. For the purposes of this book it can be defined as *'winter travelling on snow off the track or piste, by small parties, over moderate mountain terrain and wearing cross country skis.'* This, if hardly succinct, should give you a good idea of the subjects this book will deal with. Touring in the high mountains, on downhill skis, is covered in another book in this series *'Ski Mountaineering.'*

A ski-touring trip can last for a day, half a day, or for weeks on end. Ski tourers can overnight in tents, snow holes, hostels, hotels, forest shelters or mountain huts, but a level of competence out of doors is a clear pre-requisite, *and will be assumed in the readership of this book.*

WHO GOES SKI TOURING?
Ski-touring, as defined here, will obviously appeal to those cross country skiers bored with endlessly circling the XC track or *'loipe'.* Downhill skiers will find it a challenging alternative to the crowded lifts and well manicured slopes, but the total number of people who *could* go ski-touring is much wider than the snow-crowd. Mountaineers, rock climbers, walkers, hikers, hillwalkers, backpackers and campers will all find ski-touring a natural and useful extension of their normal summer sport.

These people will have much of the kit and experience necessary for ski-touring, and a fair grasp of the problems involved in winter travel.

CAN ANYONE SKI-TOUR?
The answer to that question is a qualified 'yes'. Going ski-touring and being a ski-tourer are two different things, and while doing the first will eventually transform you into the second, you should at the start be able to list among your personal resources most of the following points:-

1. Outdoor experience in hiking, hillwalking or backpacking.
2. Basic XC skiing ability.
3. Reasonable physical fitness.
4. Winter walking and camping experience.
5. Competence with map and compass.
6. Possess a range of lightweight camping equipment and winter clothing.
7. Have a knowledge of outdoor hazards and survival skills.
8. Know first aid *and* weather lore.
9. Be able to plan ahead and be companionable.
10. Have common sense.

This book is a Master Guide, and ski-touring is not for beginners. If you never go 'out-of-doors', don't start by going ski-touring. To be enjoyable, ski touring must be grounded on a sound knowledge or ability in the basic outdoor skills, for the simple reason that you ski-tour in winter and off the beaten track. This is no place for the absolute beginner. Unless you can give an affirmative answer to most of these ten points, or are prepared to improve your present knowledge until you can, then leave ski touring alone, at least for the present.

WHY GO SKI TOURING?

Ski touring on cross country skis is the natural step for anyone who enjoys the outdoors in the spring, summer or autumn. Once the first snow falls the crowds will melt away, and you will find the hills as you dream they should be and so rarely are; remote, quiet, empty, beautiful.

You can travel up to twenty miles a day on XC skis, a good distance in the short winter days, and the mountain huts or campsites are rarely crowded. Moreover, there are certain trails which are best covered in winter, or specially designed for winter travel. The *Grande Traversée* of the Jura in Eastern France is just one example of this.

XC techniques are relatively easy to learn and the basic equipment is not expensive, so that the development of summer skills and equipment up to a winter ski touring level is far from difficult in terms of cost and athletic ability.

Finally, ski touring is fun. I plead guilty to the cause of enjoyment. If you don't like it, don't do it, but this is a sport not a religion, and one in which the ability to enjoy yourself, even in adverse conditions, is a pre-requisite.

FITNESS AND TECHNIQUE

Fun it may be, but it can be hard work. This is a fact, and it is no good denying it. However, if you have an existing level of fitness founded on such summer activities as hillwalking or backpacking, you will not find the effort surprising and, it must be emphasised, good XC skiing techniques will greatly reduce the effort. Such techniques are covered in a later chapter and may be learned in a few days.

INSURANCE

Common sense is a good attribute, but things can go wrong and a little compensation is always useful. Get insurance cover for your equipment and effects and insure yourself for accident and medical care, especially before going abroad.

EXPERIENCE

You don't have to go out in the depths of winter to discover that the hills can be dangerous places for the unprepared. Experience of severe conditions in the hills, acquired during the other three seasons, is a useful step to winter skills, but not sufficient on its own. Deep winter can introduce unique conditions, either separately or in combination. Wind-chill, avalanches, frostbite and hypothermia, while not everyday events, are constant possibilities. Great skills with stove or compass in the summer are no real guarantee of similar successes in the winter hills in sub-zero temperatures. Winter skills must be acquired with caution.

EQUIPMENT
The possession of, and the ability to use lightweight backpacking or camping equipment is a great advantage, but this equipment will almost certainly need to be augmented or upgraded if you are to ski tour in safety and comfort, while extra winter equipment, crampons, ice axes, skis, and so on, must be acquired and their uses mastered.

SKILLS
Before you entertain the notion of winter travel in the hills at all you should be a competent outdoors person. To call yourself competent you must have a good grasp of:-

1. Map and compass work.
2. Survival and Rescue Techniques.
3. First Aid.
4. Weather Forecasting.
5. Camping and Cooking skills.

This book assumes that you *have* such skills and will simply show you how to apply them, plus specific winter skills as well. If you lack such skills, the *Master Guide to Outdoor Skills* will teach them to you.

PLANNING, COMPANIONS, COMMON SENSE
You cannot just go out ski touring, as you would go out for a summer afternoon's walk. If you could, there would be no challenge, and half the fun would disappear. Even a half-day ski tour must be thought out, and some prior arrangements made before you leave. Here again, as always, there are basic priorities, the ability to plan being just one of them.

It does help if you are reasonably easy to get on with. You should not go into the hills in winter on your own, and most authorities state that four people is the minimum number for any extended tour. Although I have frequently gone with just a single companion, I have NEVER gone alone. You can be cooped up together for long hours in tent or cabin, and must keep together in the day without too much ranging ahead or falling behind. So be sure you get on together and are compatable in speed and skills, or the tour can be misery.

Finally, common sense. If you have it, use it. It will save everyone a lot of trouble. If you haven't got it, well, you wouldn't be reading this book.

SKI TOUR KIT LIST
This is a suggested list, and probably too large, though leaving out such possible items as cameras and film. Study this list closely, for we will be discussing the items it contains at some length in the next few chapters. Notice that some items are, or may be carried on a group basis, so think who might make up your group. The right gear and the right group are the basic ingredients in any successful tour.

Individual

Clothes	Equipment
Down bootees	Avalanche cord
Down jacket, vest, shirt	Bindings
Face mask, balaclava.	Ski-boots
Gaiters	Bivvy Bag

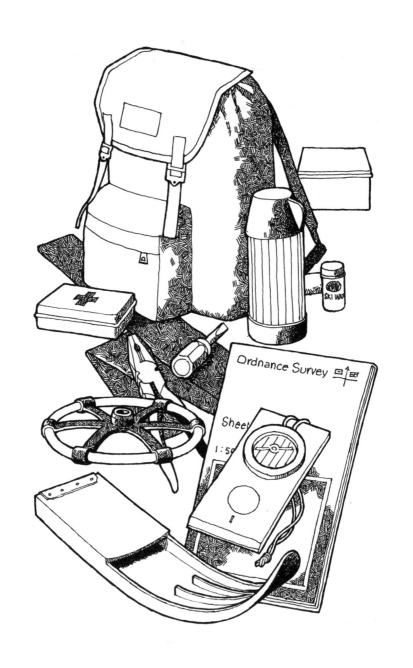

Ordnance Survey

Sheet

1:5

Gloves
Hat
Scarf
Shell clothing, cagoule, pants
Socks, stockings
Spare dry clothing (incl. gloves)
Sunglasses or goggles
Sweater
Thermal underwear
Trousers or breeches (knickers)
Washing gear

Compass
Crampons
Ice axe
Poles
Rucksack
Sleeping mat
Sleeping bag
Snow shoes
Sun cream
Torch/headlamp
XC touring skis.

Group Gear

Tent(s)	Snow shovel	Spare ski tip and
Stove(s)	Food	repair kit
Fuel	Water	Emergency flares
XC waxes	Cleaning gear	Snow shoes
Cooking pots	Maps	Lamps
First aid kit		Altimeter

The division between personal and group gear is arbitrary and depends on the group, the terrain and the objects of the trip. Weight is always a problem, so the sharing of items to reduce individual loads is essential, and another reason why the group must stay together.

One final point. I remember the story of the publisher of children's books who asked a little girl for her opinion on a book he had published on penguins. She returned it with the polite comment, *'This book tells me more about penguins than I really want to know'.*

Many books are like that. They leave the reader bloated with information, if not thoroughly confused. I have tried here to distil the essence of ski touring with enough information on all aspects to get you started, without great cost, error, or danger. Like all sports though, the true benefit must come from doing it, and I hope this book encourages you to go out and try.

This said, let us start to study ski touring, an activity which can put the winter hills, the unmarked snowfields and the high wild places within reach of your ski-tips. This is another world, quiet, beautiful, lethal, endlessly fascinating and ever-changing. Go there with confidence and good companions and you will return with memories of happy times and true and tested friendships.

2 · Ski tour clothing

Good clothing is a comfort at any time, but vital in winter. The word 'winter' covers such a variety of extremes that just to point out that winter equals cold is neither sufficient nor wholly accurate, for I have spent many days sweltering on the snowfields. Tour clothing must be adaptable in use and suitable for the wide variety of conditions you may encounter in the course of a trip.

THE PRINCIPLES OF WINTER CLOTHING
As an experienced outdoors man (or woman), you will probably possess many of these items. Winter items which you may not have but will need, include:-

Down bootees
Nylon overboots (Boot-gloves)
Facemasks or Balaclave helmet
Thermal underwear
Heel or instep crampons

Any outdoor shop stocking high mountain gear will probably carry these items, or you will soon acquire them on your travels into ski touring areas. However, and most important for your safety and comfort, let us just look at winter clothing principles.

You need suitable clothing in winter to keep you warm, and in extreme situations or climates, to keep you alive. With suitable clothing used in the correct combinations you are perfectly safe, even at well below zero temperatures.

I do not want you to think that because 'cold', 'below zero' and 'extreme' are words employed in winter, you need all this gear everywhere or all the time. It depends where you go and when, but you should understand the situations you are likely to meet and be suitably clad to cope with them.

The principle which governs warmth in winter is the 'layer' principle. This is based on the fact that two or more thin garments are warmer than one thick one, because of the 'dead' air trapped between the layers. Down provides lots of dead air space and is therefore warm, while many modern synthetics are capable of providing both dead air pace and resistance to wet. 'Thinsulate' synthetic garments with polyolefin filling are said to be extremely warm. The snow-shedding properties of proofed or 'rip-stop' nylon should also be considered when buying as melting snow can soak your garments.

The velcro-covered zip is another boon to the ski tourer, for XC skiing is hot work and the second problem you will encounter is overheating. You must aim to avoid soaking your clothes with perspiration, or at least reduce perspiration by using your zips constantly to air and cool the body. This achieved you can fight the wind with your shell clothing and wind-shirts.

FOOTWEAR

Cross country ski-boots will be covered in the next chapter, as they are, strictly speaking, an item of ski equipment. Apart from this you will require other forms of footwear, plus extra insulation to cope with low temperatures. Insulation is the key to winter warmth and the risk of frozen feet and frostbite should make you extra cautious over footwear.

All winter footwear should be roomy enough to permit the wearing of two pairs of wool socks or stockings and the insertion of insulating felt or neoprene insoles if necessary. Cold strikes up from the snow and this extra layer inside the shoe can be vital. Canvas or neoprene overboots (or mukluks) are popular for stamping around campsites, as are down bootees. All outdoor footwear should have rough or serrated soles, for the risk of a slip and a heavy fall is quite high. Down bootees are also useful to wear around the mountain hut or inside the tent. A pair of the American 'Shoepac' boots, which have rubber feet and leather legs, is a good investment, although the rubber will make the feet perspire. In more simple conditions a plastic bag secured over the foot can help keep the chill out. XC overshoes or 'boot-gloves' in proofed nylon are also useful and even newspaper insoles can make a significant difference.

My personal range of footwear is XC boots with gaiters for skiing, down bootees for the campsite, and a pair of soft leather moccasins for wear around the hut. I like warm feet and would carry extra footwear to keep them that way.

Plenty of socks are essential, but do not wear so many socks or lace the boots so tight that you constrict the foot inside the boot. This could lead to circulation loss and this in turn can lead to chilblains or frostnip. Winter equals cold and your feet are always in the snow.

BOOTS

Slips on the ice are a real menace in winter, and if much bush-whacking or climbing — of the non-alpine variety — is called for, then a pair of stout walking boots and crampons would be useful. XC boots usually have smooth soles and give little support on icy paths, so I compromise by wearing light heel or instep crampons for extra grip. Study the map before you leave and decide what footwear you will need, for just relying on your XC boots is rarely sufficient, and you may have to take the skis off and walk quite often. A waterproof dressing with some proofing compound, like Sno-seal or Wet-Proof or Nik-wax is a good idea, for this will help to keep your feet dry.

SOCKS OR STOCKINGS

Always carry more socks in the winter than you would in summer, and aim to change them often. I wear one long pair (stockings) and one short pair, in either loop-stitch, or Norwegian wool, 'Raggsox'. Wash them a couple of times before you wear them, which will soften and fluff up the wool, providing extra insulation. Keep the extremities, hands, feet, toes, fingers and ears warm, whatever you do.

UNDERWEAR

An underwear set is essential, and the basic outfit used to be a set of 'long-johns' and a string vest. This is still a popular combination, but personally I have changed all this for a set of 'Lifa' thermal underwear in polypropylene. I found that woollen long-johns were too hot and itchy and the string vest was uncomfortable under the pressure of a pack. Lifa underwear suits me very well.

Thermal underwear, in a synthetic fibre mix gives excellent insulation, without much weight or bulk, and, most important, allows perspiration to disperse or 'wick' to the outer layers, and this would be the most suitable wear for touring. A spare Lifa suit is excellent for sleeping in.

TROUSERS OR BREECHES

It is up to the individual to choose between trousers or breeches (knickers in the USA). Personally, because they are less conspicuous when I return to

civilization, I usually wear cord trousers, but I have breeches, which are useful because they have very deep pockets, handy for storing maps and other precious items.

Garments in a snow-shedding material, like Helenca, are a boon, for if the snow sticks to it, the clothing will eventually get wet. For this reason I always wear long gaiters. All garments should permit free movement, and the Nordic XC 'salopette' or set of breeches equipped with a bib like the *Rohan* range is growing in popularity.

The only real rule is NEVER WEAR JEANS. They give no wind protection, are hard to dry and are usually too tight.

ANORAKS, DUVETS, JACKETS

Unless it rains, the down-filled 'duvet' jacket in rip-stop nylon is *the* ski touring garment. If it rains and the down clogs, then the garment is useless, and (an initial thought), down is increasingly expensive. Synthetic-filled duvets, in *Hollofil, Fibrefill II,* or some other material are often preferred for they are cheaper than down and give insulation, even when wet. You can also get good protection from a fibre-pile jacket, and other garments worth considering are down vests and shirts, light proofed nylon and wind-shirts and wind-pants, or a ventile jacket of 'parka'. While you are moving, ski-touring is hot work, but the 'layer' principle must be applied to your choice of garments. If the wind is blowing, and it usually is, you need to put on something wind-proof as soon as you stop or you will chill rapidly. The best combination is a range of zippered garments, which you can change at will, with a duvet jacket and windproofs for when you stop or for extreme

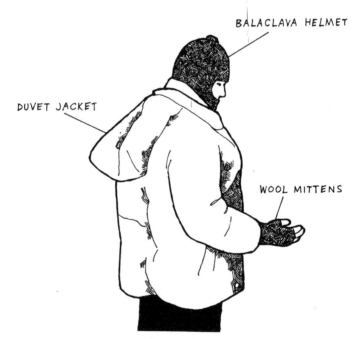

BALACLAVA HELMET

DUVET JACKET

WOOL MITTENS

conditions. A down vest with zip-in sleeves, is the perfect XC combination. All XC jackets should have hoods.

My current wear is a hooded fibre-pile K2 jacket, with a down vest as well if this proves insufficient, and a set of windproofs. I have taken this assortment into a variety of situations and it has served me well.

All ski-jackets should ideally have the following features:- Hoods; pop-down flaps to keep the ice and snow off the zips or velcro strips; good deep flapped pockets; 'hand-warmer' pockets behind the side pockets. The jacket should be hip length, and a draw-string at the waist or bottom hem can be handy in a high wind, if inhibiting to the ski-ing.

SHIRTS, SWEATERS
Many synthetic materials are good but in my opinion wool is best. Choose shirts, ski sweaters or wool pullovers which are long and loose fitting. Keep the chill air away from the neck, wrists and the small of the back, and you will feel much more comfortable. Cotton roll-neck sweaters are very popular.

HATS, GLOVES, FACEMASKS
A hat and gloves are essential in the winter. The hat should protect the ears, or even the face from the wind. For this reason the woollen 'balaclava' helmet is often worn. If you buy a balaclava, get one with a peak which will shade your eyes and protect them from twigs when bushwacking. The head is the body's radiator and some 30% of body heat loss is from that area alone, so if you get hot take your hat off. If you feel cold, put it on.

The winter winds can flay exposed skin in minutes and the face and lips can get very chapped. To apply a good moisture barrier cream is essential, but if the winds are really blowing, protect yourself with a facemask which I prefer to the itchy balaclava.

A light silk or nylon or suede facemask with a cotton mouthpatch which absorbs breath moisture, worn with a ski hat, is my own choice for the below zero wind-chill conditions.

Whether you choose gloves or mittens is a personal choice. I wear loose ski-gloves, in leather, with cotton inner gloves for extra insulation. These gloves zip up over the wrists of my duvet jacket and seal them from the snow, so keeping the wrist veins covered and the blood warm. Wherever the blood runs close to the skin needs protection.

Dachstein mitts are a very good buy and you can get 'Polarguard' mitts with slits in the thumb and palm to let your fingers out for any fiddly job. I prefer gloves, but if you are a mitt-man I don't blame you.

GOGGLES, GLASSES, CREAMS
Snow glare can be blinding, so carry goggles or glasses wide enough to shield the eyes from the sun's glare on the snow. I prefer goggles, but many tourers use glasses. Do carry and use a lip salve and a barrier cream. Beards can be a problem in extreme cold conditions since they and the skin underneath can hardly be protected.

WINDPROOFS
Summer walkers and backpackers carry 'shell' clothing, or waterproofs, in case it rains. This is what such garments are commonly for.

However, the essential feature of these garments is that they are, or should be windproof, and the ski tourer will quickly discover just how necessary windproofs are, for the wind in winter is a chiller and a killer. These garments are commonly in proofed nylon, but *Goretex* fabric, which lets perspiration escape, seems very effective in cold, dry conditions.

The windproof suit consists of a hooded 'cagoule', a set of over-trousers and gaiters. For ski-touring use the cagoule which has a full-length zip, flapped and sealed with velcro, and is most suitable as it permits ventilation. The hood should have a wire stiffened face-piece for wind protection. A waist draw-cord is also useful, but a hem cord can, if tightened, inhibit the diagonal stride. All pockets should be zipped and flapped, or they will fill with snow or water.

Over-trousers should be elasticated at the waist, with legs wide enough to slip on over boots and trousers. Flapped zips should secure the leg gussets, and they should fit closely at the ankle, but over the gaiters, which will keep snow from slipping down inside the gaiters and wetting the feet.

I wear gaiters all the time. They help to keep the feet and legs dry, provide extra insulation and, a useful point, can provide padding for the ankles against the crusty snow if you are running downhill with the skis just submerged. I prefer the sort of gaiter which you can unzip to remove completely, so that I can use it as a 'sitz-mat' during a lunch break. The zips can freeze but a rub of salt will usually release them.

SPARE CLOTHING

At night, in the tent or hut, it is useful and pleasant to change into dry, warm clothing, and allow your touring clothes to dry and air as much as possible. In addition you must carry spare clothing, in case you get really wet during the day. In summer if you get wet you stay wet. In winter in the high hills, you have to change into dry garments or you can freeze, so spare clothes are essential.

A track suit, spare socks and a scarf are a sufficient minimum with a pair of soft shoes or moccasins, to fill the bill in most situations.

CLEANING AND CLOTHES CARE

Well washed and clean clothes are warmer than unwashed ones. On long tours the chance to wash the body, never mind the clothes, is a rare event, and if you are out for a week or more, it is a good idea to stop somewhere for a day to have a good clean up and replenish stores, with a bath for you and a washing day for your very '*doggy*' garments. Most ski tourers return to base in a highly scented state, but fortunately since everyone is in the same state, nobody complains very much.

Packing away sweaty, unwashed garments, even for a few days, is a bad idea, so separate all the clothing and have it washed or dry cleaned at once.

Down garments should be washed as little as possible, but since they do get dirty, a once-a-year bath could be useful. Preparations like '*Fluffy*' or '*Soppy*' are available for washing down, and my method is to soak the garment in '*Soppy*' solution for several hours in a bath of lukewarm water, turning and kneading it constantly until the dirt has been eased out. I then spin it in the washing machine to get the water out and finish it off in the dryer. The down will be matted into lumps and takes longer to dry, but you can separate these lumps and spread the down along the sections, shaking the garment constantly. Handle the wet garment with care, as the wet heavy down can tear the 'baffles' between the compartments. If you have your sleeping bag dry cleaned, beware of cleaning fluid fumes and air the bag thoroughly before you use it again.

A needle and thread or 'rip-stop' tape are useful items to carry on the trail. You don't need to make elegant repairs, just something to get you back to base.

When you do get back, wash the clothes, check for fraying seams, wash off or sponge out any mud, and let your clothes dry and air thoroughly.

Good quality garments, which are the only sort suitable for ski-touring, are not cheap and it makes good sense to look after them.

3 · Ski touring equipment

By the time you contemplate ski touring you will have acquired many of the items needed for a successful tour, apart perhaps from the skis and certain items of winter clothing and equipment. This will include at least some of the following items.

Rucksacks	Torch, lamp, candles (g)
Ice axe	Survival kit (g)
Crampons	Avalanche cord or sonde
Stove (g)	First aid kit (g)
Sleeping bag	Tent (g)
Sleeping mat	Water bottle
Compass (g)	Repair kit (g)
Snowshoes	Flares (g)
Shovel (g)	

(g) = group or shared items.

This list is simply a list of 'headings'. Many items are optional. You may well have such equipment, but it may not be entirely or even at all suitable for ski-touring, so in this chapter we will look at your outdoor equipment, examining its suitability for winter in general and ski touring in particular. Please note that wherever possible 'group' items are carried to help reduce individual weight.

RUCKSACKS

The normal framed backpacker's rucksack is not suitable for ski touring. You can manage with it but, as a rule, they are too big, too wide, and designed to carry the weight too high.

The ideal ski touring sac is narrow, consisting of a single compartment without side pockets. Side pockets impede the arm action of the cross country skier. A top-flap pocket though is useful. It is frameless, or with a very light integral frame, which fits close and comfortably to the back, secured against swinging with a hip harness and, if possible, a chest or 'sternum' strap to stop the shoulder straps slipping. When loading a ski touring sac, the weighty items, tent, stove, fuel, should go at the bottom, the aim being to keep the weight low and help the skier keep in balance. The sac itself should be of a snow-proof material, with zipped and flapped apertures, and the bottom, which will often rest in the snow, should be completely waterproof, in suede or double proofed Cordura nylon. If the sac *has* side pockets these should either be removable or not protrude too far. Ice axe loops, a crampon patch and ski straps or pockets are also necessary and are essential features on a ski touring sac.

There are a great many ski touring sacs on the market, and such manufacturers as *Berghaus* (UK), *Lowe Alpine* (US), *Millet* (France) and *Bergan* (Norway) are leading international names among a wide range of rivals. Go to a leading equipment supplier and study the outdoor magazines to decide on a suitable sac. Try it on *loaded.* The difference in balance is critical and it must fit well under load. Fill it with gas cylinders and you get a good idea of the loaded weight and balance.

Sac size is a problem for it depends on the distance you have to cover, the weather, the terrain and where you intend to stay. The more permanent the accommodation the less you need to carry. You can use a smaller sac on a DNT hut tour of Norway, but you need a large sac for a ski backpacking trip in the Tetons of the USA. Personally I think a 60 litre sac is the *maximum* sensible size. Sacs like the *Lowe Alpine* range, which have side pressure straps and can therefore reduce or expand their capacity at will, are ideal.

Few people want, or can afford, a wide range of ski touring sacs. Your choice will depend on where you tour, but it is sound advice to buy a sac as large as you will ever need, but never carry more in it than you can help.

ICE AXE

Many ski tourers do not carry ice axes, but I believe that anyone who goes into the winter hills should carry one and know how to cut steps and brake with it. Apart from the safety aspect an ice axe can serve as a super peg for main tent guys. Ski tourers can make the ice axe particularly useful by fitting a ski-basket over the shaft at the spike end; XC tours often involve walking down icy or non ski-able slopes. Your ski poles will be very useful

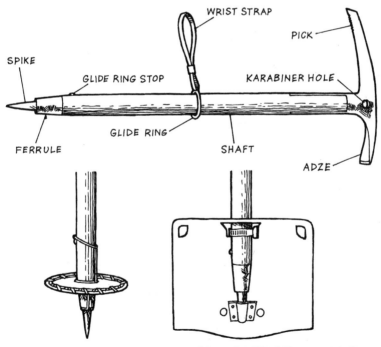

SNOW BASKET ATTACHMENT   SNOW SHOVEL ATTACHED TO ICE AXE

as support, but an ice axe gives real security. A walking axe, with a shaft of about 70-75cm. length (30ins.) is about right. This would be too long for ice climbing but fills the bill in most other situations. A wrist sling should be fitted, and step cutting and braking should be practised regularly.

CRAMPONS
The same holds for proper crampons. A pair of heel or instep crampons can be useful for walking around, even in a village but proper hill crampons are better. They should be carried by anyone in the winter hills, for some ice walking is always a possibility.

Ten-point crampons are best for general use, apart from ice climbing, but correct fitting is essential. Check, by shaking the foot hard, that the crampons will not fall off or wobble on the boot. *Salewa* is just one good reliable make.

STOVE
A stove can be a group item. Stove fuel and cook pots shared among the group members will lessen individual weight. Butane, the most popular liquid gas, will not 'gasify' in winter unless used in a stove with a pre-heat device. Of the alternative fuels, propane containers are heavy, solid fuel slow and gives off fumes, and meths, while giving adequate heat, tends to be a slow cooking medium, and the most popular meths stove, the *Trangia,* is thirsty, and you therefore need a lot of fuel to use it.

This said, the *Trangia* is an excellent stove, with few parts to go wrong, so if you don't have much need for a stove, on a hut-tour say, then take a *Trangia*.

The best fuels for the winter are paraffin (kerosene) or white gas (unleaded petrol). Popular makes of stoves using such fuels are the *Svea,* the *Primus* or the *Optimus* range. Buy a stove with a wind shield, a simmering control and a self-pricking device. A pump will help build pressure at low temperatures, and when buying the stove it is sensible to buy a funnel and a few spare nipples and washers. Petrol stoves can be dangerous, so they should be filled, lit and used with care. A tent or hut fire can be especially hazardous in winter.

SLEEPING BAG
As every catalogue will tell you, the secret of a warm bag lies in the

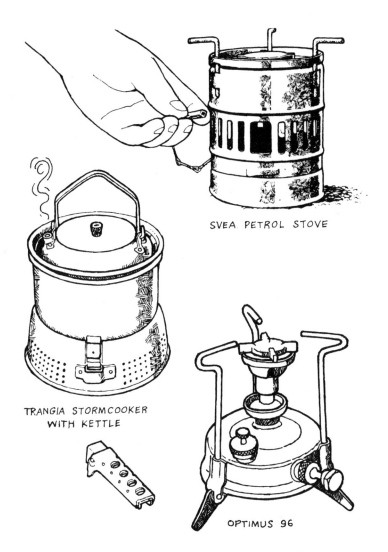

SVEA PETROL STOVE

TRANGIA STORMCOOKER
WITH KETTLE

OPTIMUS 96

construction as well as the filling. Of the various methods of construction the slant wall construction, with differential cut, is said to be the warmest and is certainly the most popular. Down bags are now very expensive, but if you can be *sure* of cold dry weather, and a dry pitch, there is nothing to beat down, which is light and less bulky than any synthetic. In less reliable climes, a synthetic filled bag is more useful since they are warm even when wet, and if you are tenting on your tour then a synthetic bag is the best since it is almost impossible to keep the tent dry inside.

Bag selection is largely a matter of personal choice, and, as an experienced outdoorsman, you may have a suitable winter or high mountain bag already. For hut use these may be too warm, but it is usually better to be too warm than too cold and not many people can afford a range of bags. Buy a bag rated down to − 20°F and you should have one suitable for most conditions. The 'mummy' bag is very warm, but some people find them too constricting. Full length zips provide a 'cold spot' in the bag, but on the other hand if it gets really cold, you can zip two bags together and share body warmth. The covering fabric should be a hard wearing rip-stop nylon and you should carry the bag in a nylon stuff sack to keep it dry and free from sweat.

As to filling weight, provided the construction is helpful, the lighter the better. Down is lighter than synthetic, but even so a touring bag should hold at least 3 lb of down. To get equivalent protection from a synthetic bag you will need at least 5 lb. of filling and synthetic filled bags tend to be bulkier than down, but the development of outdoor gear is proceeding at such a pace that some equally light, compact and effective synthetic may appear at any moment. Please consider though that a ski touring trip is not the place to try out some new 'wonder' bag. If it lets you down you are in for sleepless nights or real trouble. It will help if your bag has a hood. When you turn in put on dry clothes, or a spare set of 'Lifa', but do not get into the bag in your day wear. It is sure to be damp either from snow of perspiration. Zips can freeze, even inside a tent so be sure they are covered or you might have trouble getting up.

SLEEPING MATS
Air beds are out! They are heavy, prone to leak, and when inflated, force you to lie on cold air. Use a full length closed cell pad, of ⅜″ thickness or more, and pack as much insulation as possible under the mat on the bottom of the tent, or on the snow surface. Self-inflating foam pads, like the *Thermarest* are very good, very warm and take up less room than the foam cell mattress.

MAP AND COMPASS
Never go out in winter without both map and compass, and use both all the time. Winter map reading is complicated by poor visibility and the changed shapes of features due to snow cover. Trail marks and cairns can be hidden under the snow, so good map and compass work is essential. A good orienteering compass and maps of 1:25000 metric scale or equivalent are essential. If you are touring abroad, away from your summer stamping ground, don't overlook the obvious. I was intrigued to discover that *one* Norwegian mile was the equivalent of *six* English miles! Half a Norwegian mile is 5 kilometres! The compass variation or declination in North America can vary from 25° West to 25° East. Don't assume it is the one you are used to. Your life can depend on good off-trail navigation.

SNOW SHOES
Snow shoes are often used as an alternative to skis for cross country touring. Even for committed XC ski tourers they can come in useful for bushwacking, or for moving around the campsite where long skis can be a considerable disadvantage. For such occasional use the big *'Green Mountain'* or *'Bear Paw'* snowshoes — about 10″ wide by 36″ long — are

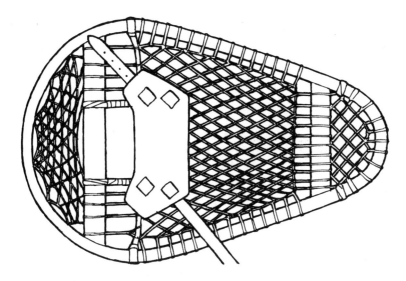

too large. A small pair of 'racquettes' about the size of large tennis rackets, will serve. These are light, often made of alloy with neoprene webbing and, strapped to your rucksack, will cause no problems.

SNOW SHOVEL

This, again, can be a group item, but if you are going snow-holing, then one shovel between two people is about right. Digging a snow-hole without a shovel is a long job and hard work, so a light folding snow shovel is useful as a group safety item on a tent or hut tour and essential on a one-between-two scale if you intend to snow-hole. The manufacturers of *Rottefella* bindings, Witco, make a very good one.

LIGHTS

Torches, while useful, are awkward. The best form of torch, which leaves the hands free and shines the beam where you want it, is the head lamp. The cold tends to weather the batteries rather quickly so carry spares and keep them warm. For hut or tent use, long-life candles are useful and can serve for emergency fire lighting. Use them with care, either in a candle lantern or a cook pot and beware of fire. In a snow-hole, thanks to the reflection of the crystals, one small candle is like a floodlight. They also give off a useful amount of warmth.

SURVIVAL KIT

I am a belt-and-braces outdoorsman and although this book assumes experience, I have no idea just how experienced you are. As a matter of common sense, every tourer should carry, on at least a group basis, the *Ten Essentials* — and know how to use them. These are:-

1. A local map of not less than 1:50,000 scale.
2. A compass. You must know how to use both map and compass.

3. A spare warm sweater, socks and overtrousers.
4. A small pack of high-calorie food. Chocolate, glucose, biscuits, all have high calorific content. Food is the fuel that keeps you warm.
5. A plastic sheet, 1 metre (3' 3") wide by 3 metres (10') long, or a plastic survival bag.
6. A 'space' blanket.
7. A whistle.
8. Matches.
9. Torch.
10. Candle.

You may carry these anyway, but remember they have a "safety" role as well. It might also be sensible to carry some emergency flares, or coloured smoke canisters, but these would be a 'group' item.

AVALANCHE CORD OR SONDE

If more off-piste downhill skiers and ski tourers used an avalanche cord, there would be fewer deaths in avalanches. The cord consists simply of a 50ft. or 100ft. length or red line with direction markers every five feet, weighing about 3oz. If you are swept under by an avalanche, this cord will float to the surface and enable the rescuers to find you. All you have to do when crossing any tricky slope, is to tie the cord around your waist and trail it behind you.

The sonde is a more sophisticated method, with each skier carrying a small electrical device, the sonde, which transmits a 'bleep' to rescuers on the surface. A *'Pieps'* sonde is a fairly standard system and can be hired from most ski touring shops.

XC ski tourers do not always tour in avalanche terrain, but an avalanche can happen anywhere, so if your chosen area has any record of avalanches, take a cord or hire a sonde, and use it.

FIRST AID KIT

This can also be carried on a group basis. It can contain the same items as the best summer one, with extra supplies of lip salve, 'glacier' face cream and salt tablets, and crepe bandages.

TENT

Tents present a problem. Many areas have hut systems so tents are unnecessary. Alan Blackshaw took a tent on his Arctic tour, over two winters, but according to the report *"very rarely used it"* — and he was awarded the Perry Medal. However, there are areas where a tent is the only answer, so just be sure the one you take is up to the conditions.

If you have a good wind-shedding backpacking tent, this will probably serve very well for most of your ski tours, and in many countries it is neither necessary nor even advisable to use tents at all, except in an emergency. Snow can be heavy, so the tent should shed it, with steep sides and a steady ridge pole or bracing. Tunnel or dome tents are good, especially if you link up the tunnels between the tents, to keep the group in contact.

Given that your tent has a flysheet, and a deep waterproof tray base, the ski touring tent is light, but must be large enough to contain *all* your gear. Gear left out will freeze or disappear under the snow. The fabric should be of rip-stop proofed nylon and shaped to shed wind. Adequate guy lines are essential and the fly should be capable of close pegging to the snow, and equipped with a wide side flap, or 'snow valance' to keep the tent stable. Your normal backpacking tent may need some customising for snow use, and sewing on extra guy lines and fitting a fabric 'frost-liner' would be two useful steps. A wide range of pegs to cope with anything from ice to slush should be carried.

WATER BOTTLE
You may find that water is quite hard to come by on the snowfields. You *can* melt snow, but it's a slow business and it takes a bucket of snow to yield a cup of water. You can speed it up a little by using water to dissolve the snow as you melt it or, even better melt ice. Ski touring is thirsty work, so you will certainly need to carry water. In extreme cold, carry the bottle upside down in the sac so that any ice forms at the bottom, and does not clog the neck. At night you must take the bottles into the tent, or even into the sleeping bags. Your last task at night and at the end of every meal, is to melt some snow for water at the next meal.

REPAIR KIT
Modern skis are tough but if you use them hard they can fracture. A spare ski-tip should always be carried. Binding screws need to be checked, and you should carry spare screws, a screwdriver, and some epoxy or swift act glue. If you pop a screw you will need shelter to repair the binding — so the tent can be handy. Fill the hole with glue and maybe a match stick and screw it up tight. Hold the binding upside down so that the glue sets around the head. Be wary of fast setting glues for you can stick your fingers together very rapidly. Apart from these items you should carry some wire, a spare binding clamp or wish bone, and some insulating tape.

Finally, please note again, that it is not necessary to carry all this equipment all the time. It depends on what you are doing, where and when.

However, until you know when to carry this gear and how to use it, if necessary, you will not be a competent ski tourer.

4 · Skiing equipment

BOOTS, BINDINGS, POLES, SKIS

Cross country equipment is light. Ski touring work is hard. It follows therefore that the equipment must be strong and designed by experts for the job it has to do. Cross country equipment is now much more sophisticated than it was even five years ago, and there is no doubt that further variety and technical innovations will continue to appear and further fog the scene.

Do not skimp on equipment but buy the best you can afford. It will be cheaper in the long run. Fortunately cross country gear is (relatively) inexpensive and if you look after it the gear will last for years. We will concentrate on the touring side and go through the equipment item by item to note the points to look out for when buying.

BOOTS

At present, and for the foreseeable future, the best XC boots come from Norway. Insist on Norwegian or at least Scandinavian boots, which fit British and American feet well, and you will be on the right track. Most boots are produced to the *Nordic Norm*, which ensures that any boot will fit any binding. For touring the 'Norm' is 75mm across the toe binding. Racing and light touring boots are cut to below the ankle bone, but ski-touring boots are cut above. All touring boots should have cowhide uppers, treated to resist the wet. The soles are of rubber or polyurethane. The sole should flex easily, but is stiffened with a steel or wood instep shank to resist lateral distortion. The flange on the toe should contain pin-holes for the binding and these holes should have a metal sleeve. The heel should be grooved to hold the cable of a binding. Noted manufcturers are *Suvernen, Edsbyn, Adidas, Trak, Lake Placid, Risport, Perssons.*

When going to buy boots, take with you, or borrow from the shop, the normal two pairs of socks, one thick long pair and a short, thinner pair. A boot must fit well, and wearing the normal amount of socks will ensure a correct purchase.

A cross country boot looks rather like a running or boxing shoe, but if you examine it carefully it has, or should have, some special features. The sole at the toe projects into a wide extended flap. On the underside at this point, holes are drilled into the sole. These are to take the pins on the binding, and it is better if each hole is fitted with a brass sleeve, which stops the hole from becoming ragged or filling in with grit.

Now flex the sole. The heel should bend up with supple ease but there should be no sideways movement. Try and twist the instep. It should be impossible, for the steel or wood shank will give rigidity against any lateral play. Without this support your foot will slip off the ski in the turns.

The touring boot is single-skinned, often lined with fur pile with a snow cuff at the ankle, light and (thank goodness) comfortable. There should be

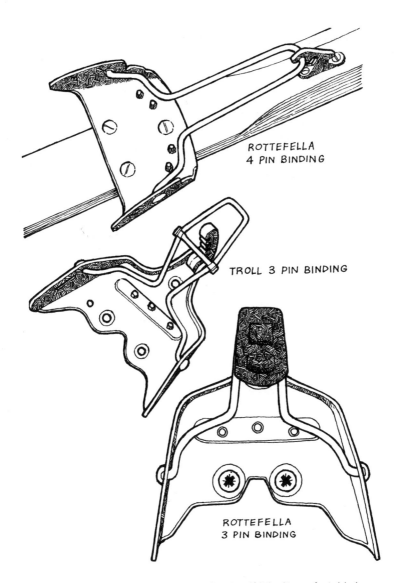

ROTTEFELLA
4 PIN BINDING

TROLL 3 PIN BINDING

ROTTEFELLA
3 PIN BINDING

no question of 'breaking in' a cross country boot — if it isn't comfortable in the shop, try another pair. If you push your foot well forward there should be room for your forefinger between the boot and your heel.

Notice that the boot is single skinned. Although silicone treated it will eventually let in the wet, and for this reason you need to wear gaiters and two pairs of socks. You should also treat the boot lightly with some water-repellent preparation like *Wet-Prufe* or *Sno-seal*. The snag is that if it is made truly water-repellent, this prevents the foot from breathing, and perspiration gets the feet wet anyway.

BINDINGS

As with boots, the choice of binding depends on the type of XC skiing you want. For general or light touring the most common and successful binding currently in use is the three-pin 'Nordic' type by *Rottefella, Kahru, Skilom* or *Troll.* In these, three metal pins in the front of the binding fit into the holes in the boot sole. The binding clamp is then forced down over a spring ratchet, and the toe is clamped securely to the ski. These are produced to the 'Nordic Norm' in standard widths of 71mm (children), 75mm and 79mm (large). The 75mm is the most popular. A new 50mm touring binding is also becoming available from leading manufacturers such as *Trak.*

Other types of binding, notably by *Adidas,* and another 'Norm' the 'Racing Norm' can also be found. The great advantage of sticking to the Nordic Norm is that any boot fits any binding, so if something breaks, replacement does not involve a complete change of gear.

Although the heel can rise, there is also a serrated metal or plastic heel plate, which is situated on the ski, directly under the heel. This will grip the boot heel when your weight is down, for turning or stopping. The heel plate should also have a central 'popper' which keeps snow from building up under the heel.

Most toe bindings are a standard 75mm size, which will fit most boots. If your feet are very large or very small, you may need to order the 71mm or 79mm size. Note that there is a left and right binding and they are usually so marked. A correctly fitted binding is set just behind the balance point so that the ski-tips hang down.

CABLES AND CLAMPS

Most cable bindings have latches which enable the cable to be braced, so clamping the heel down and forcing the toe into the binding. This has no safety release and if you fall, watch out! However, many XC tourers like cable bindings and you should know that they exist. My opinion is this. Firstly, a fall in a clamped cable binding can break your leg. Secondly, if this happens on a long tour you are in real trouble. It happened to a lady I know only three miles from the Scottish resort of Aviemore. She broke both legs and took seven hours before she was rescued and taken to hospital. Pain! Thirdly, (in my opinion) cables are unnecessary. Fourthly, while some maintain that cables *are* necessary for long tours, I have read many recent reports of long tours over wild country where the tourers used toe bindings, so the cables-for-rugged-country claims are best debatable. So, for my tours, no cables.

One device which *could* prove helpful is the heel clamp or *'bloc talon'.* This is a spring loaded metal ratchet, which clamps the heel down for the descent. It will hold against buffeting or a controlled fall, but springs loose if you overdo it, or fall hard. The *'bloc-talon'* is no substitute for good technique, but it is a help.

Many downhill skiers taking up XC worry about the lack of a cable or clamp to secure the boot heel down for descending, turning or stopping. Cable bindings by *Tempo* or *Silvretta* are available and some folk prefer them, claiming that the presence of the cable helps manoeuvring. The choice is yours.

32

POLES

Until quite recently all cross country poles were of Tonkin bamboo. Bamboo poles are still available, inexpensive and very popular. However, having nearly impaled myself when a bamboo pole splintered under me, I have purchased, at moderate cost, a duraluminium pair, and I recommend you to do likewise. Fibreglass poles are coming onto the market and they are said to be excellent, but prone to collapse if treated roughly, and they get chipped.

Cross country poles are long. To be the right length they should fit comfortably into the armpit, like crutches, or a little shorter for touring. They should be light in weight, yet strong enough to support you weight while you cross a fence or obstacle. My aluminium poles are now quite curvy but give good support.

The straps should be adjustable and worn under the palms and over the backs of the wrist. The ferrule tip is slanted forward to ease exiting from the snow as you glide through. The snap-on baskets are usually of plastic, often fairly large for touring for greater support off the track or in deep snow. The holes should be wide enough to let the snow slip off easily, and this is important as the sheer weight of snow on the baskets can be quite tiring. New basket shapes are constantly being introduced, quite different from the traditional style, and the butterfly and cone baskets are very effective, both for grip and snow-shedding.

SKIS

Even more than with the downhill variety, you could have a whole book on cross country skis alone. There are currently more than 200 different models on the market, from nearly 50 manufacturers. About half the models are non-wax skis. We have already defined the sort of skiing we intend to do as touring, which narrows the choice somewhat, but the decision on which skis to use has some crucial long term effects.

WHICH TYPE OF SKI?

The type of ski you need will depend on the type of skiing you want, so first decide:-

1. If you enjoy backpacking and winter camping.
2. Would you prefer prepared trails, or off-piste deep snow?
3. Do you want to go on one-day or extended tours?
4. Which sort of terrain will you commonly ski over? Downland, hills, woods, fells, mountains?
5. What is your standard of fitness?

Until quite recently, all cross country skis were made of wood, and all wood needs tarring and waxing. Then along came synthetic skis, in came fibreglass, plastics and polyethylene, which still needs waxing but with less base preparation. Now there are skis with so-called non-wax surfaces and, if you buy these your waxing problems are considerably reduced. BUT . . . and there is always a 'but', it is undisputed, or at least conceded, that at present well waxed skis perform better than the non-waxed variety, certainly for racing, and with more reservations, for touring.

It is therefore likely that if you start cross country skiing and like it you will want to do better and go faster, which probably means waxing. But then what do you do with your step-cut non-wax skis? Let us lay out the broad pros and cons for both wax and non-wax types, and you can decide for yourself. To wax, or not to wax, or perhaps to wax a little . . .

There are, basically, three sorts of cross country skiing, and four sorts of skis, differentiated by weight and width.

RACING SKIS

Racing is self-explanatory. Racing is over prepared loipe or trails. Racing skis are very light, around 3lb. (1.5 kilos) the pair, and made of fibreglass. They are narrow, say around 44mm, and certainly less than 50mm (2") wide at the binding, and naturally quite fragile. They are too light for general cross country work and may be discounted for our purposes.

LIGHT TOURING SKIS

These are the most popular skis, accounting for between 50 and 70% of the market. They vary between 48mm and 55mm in width at the waist and weigh around 4-5lb. (2-2.5 kilos) the pair, and are the best ski for the good skier, especially if the bulk of the skiing is on prepared trails or over moderate country. Such skis are manufactured by *Splitkein, Bonna, Skilom, Kahue, Trak,* and 'downhill' firms such as *Atomic,* and *Rossignol.*

GENERAL TOURING SKIS

If you want to concentrate on climbing hills, or bashing through the woods off prepared trails, then these are the skis for you. They are fairly wide; between 52-60mm (2.25"). As they are wider they give better support in really deep soft snow, and as they are heavier and stiffer some beginners find them easier to manage on the turns. Once you have picked up the technique, they can feel a little cumbersome, weighing anything from 5lb to 7lb (3 kilos) the pair.

MOUNTAIN SKIS

A sub-division of the G-T ski is the mountain ski. Mountain skis are for off-loipe touring and even, with the correct binding, for ski mountaineering.

I have two pairs, one by *Trak* and one by *Vandel,* and looking in last year's diary I find that I used them more often than my lighter pairs.

A mountain ski will be around 55mm-58mm at the waist, in laminated hardwood or fibreglass, and filled with whole or partial steel edges for ice work. They can be wax or non-wax. Mountain skis are manufactured by such companies as *Bonna, Trak, Vandel, Fischer, Lovett* and *Edsbyn.* If you have some grasp of Alpine techniques, side steppng, stem-turns and like downhill running on open slopes, then Mountain skis could suit you very well.

As you can see, the choice of equipment is governed by the type of cross country skiing you have in mind. If we assume that one starts the sport by touring on tracks or across moderate country, developing thereafter into longer cross country expeditions with a backpack, then you need to look at touring or mountain skis, and in my opinion the 'general touring' or mountain types are the best for ski touring.

SKIING SURFACES

The cross country ski market is in a state of expansion and continual change with new techniques and materials being introduced all the time. In every case the trend is towards finding a way to avoid waxing, or at least

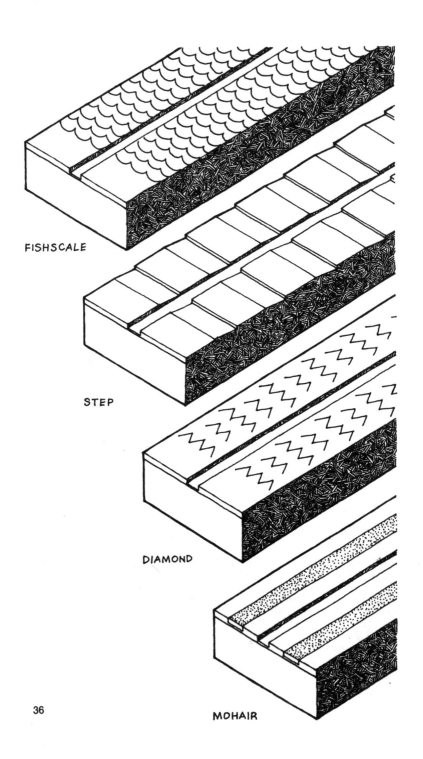

FISHSCALE

STEP

DIAMOND

MOHAIR

36

reduce it to 'running' waxes. Let me briefly explain that there are basically two sorts of waxes. 'Running' waxes give you grip which you 'kick', yet permit you to slide. 'Base' waxes hold the running wax to the ski, or to the base preparation necessary with wooden soled skis. 'Glide' waxes, a type of running wax, is necessary on all synthetic based skis. We will cover all this in more detail later, but this will make what follows more comprehensible.

Please bear with me throughout, on the thorny subject of nomenclature. The same items are called different names by different authorities, and can vary from country to country, while definitions, even when identical, can be defining different things.

I will try to *either* define any name or reference, *or* use the most self-explanatory phrase.

Broadly speaking ski bases come in four basic materials:-

1. *Wood:* The best wooden skis are made from birch, or hickory, usually laminated and edged with lignostone, a hardwood formed from compressed beech. Wood absorbs water unless protected so with a wooden-soled ski the full wax treatment is required, which consists of tarring the wood surface, then applying the appropriate waxing, corking down the running waxes etc. Tar-treated wood holds wax well, and the skis look very beautiful. I imagine, though, that they will slowly disappear or become very costly. It is, of course, possible to get a wooden ski with a plastic or P-tex bottom, which combines appearance with simplicity in waxing.

2. *Synthetic Surfaces:* More and more synthetic-soled skis are being produced, in wood, fibreglass or plastic.

The most popular material is Polyethylene, commonly called P-tex. P-tex wears fast so the skis must be soled with a high grade compound like P-tex 2000 and should have steel edges. P-tex holds wax well but many synthetic skis are also available in non wax models, with step-cut, fishscale or mohair strip patterns.

NON-WAX SKIS (STEP-CUT)
The non-wax ski is a comparatively new development and one which largely accounts for the boom in XC skiing in recent years. Such skis have indentations cut in the sole, making a 'step' or 'fishscale' pattern, usually stretching for about a metre under the foot. These patterns grip the snow when you are 'kicking' and yet still permit a smooth 'glide' over the surface when you move forward. The makers claim that they grip well and need no waxing, which up to a point is true. They work very well in 'Klister' conditions (page 44) but are less effective in powder snow or ice. Running on packed snow they make a considerable noise, and in my opinion, need some paraffin glide wax on tip and tail to reduce drag.

MOHAIR STRIPS
This is a variation on the step-cut idea, and is taken from the climbing 'skins' once popular with ski mountaineers. Thin mohair strips are let into the base of the ski and they provide a good grip, wear well and can be easily replaced. I find they are a little less effective in providing a clean glide than step-cut skis, but they work very well in temperatures 10°F either side of freezing. The mohair will freeze if it gets wet, unless sprayed with an antifreeze preparation like WD40.

MICA

Mica soled skis are the latest development. A typical mica sole has mica particles embedded into a polyethylene base. The particles are arranged to permit forward glide while gripping the snow if you slide backwards. It is claimed that mica bases work as well as correctly waxed skis. My experience is that they work very well except perhaps in fresh snow. I took mine out in a snow storm and they 'balled up' completely with fresh snow welded to the sole. I applied some hard silver wax which worked well and I got back without further trouble.

So, after deciding on ski type your basic choice is:

Wax	Wood
	Polyethylene & its derivatives (Plastic)
Non-wax	Step-cut, fishscale etc.
	Mohair-strip
	Mica-based

XC CONSTRUCTION

Skis are constructed in four different ways and although we are concerned here simply with touring skis, some knowledge of construction will be helpful.

WOOD OR PLASTIC LAMINATED

Wood laminated skis are the traditional models, comprised of up to twenty laminated layers. Plastic laminates are similar in construction, but lighter.

REINFORCED FIBREGLASS

This is a wooden ski, or of a wood and plastic or foam construction, but reinforced with a layer of fibreglass.

FIBREGLASS SANDWICH

Most skis currently available are of fibreglass sandwich construction. As the name implies it consists of an upper and lower layer of fibreglass sandwiching layers of wood, plastic or foam.

TORSION BOX

Torsion box construction exists when the laminated skis are completely wrapped, top, bottom and sides, in a fibreglass box.

TOURING SKI CONSTRUCTION

Fibreglass sandwich skis are the most common and if they are from a reputable manufacturer would be a very good buy, but beware of poor finish on unknown makes.

Foam skis, filled with plastic, are not tough enough, but torsion box construction is very tough indeed. A fibreglass sandwich or torsion box ski, of between 54mm to 58mm width at the waist would be ideal.

SHOVEL AND SIDE CUT

If you stand an alpine ski on its tail you will notice a pronounced narrowing about half way down, at the 'waist'.

This is called 'side-cut', and is an aid to downhill turning, a very important feature in an alpine ski. It is, however, less important in XC, and most racing skis are 'parallel' cut, without that narrowing at the waist.

This feature is appearing on touring skis. The side-cut allows the front, or 'shovel' of the ski to flex, and carve away the snow as you turn, and I personally find this helpful. Carrying a pack eliminates fancy footwork, but as a sometime alpine skier I recommend that your touring skis should have side-cut and a reasonable but not excessive amount of flex at the shovel. So, what is reasonable and what is excessive? If you bend back the tip and the shovel bends softly and well back towards the waist, then the shovel is too soft. Pick something firmer. A very soft shovel under load will be constantly digging under on the traverse, and some mountain skis are very soft indeed, so check this point carefully before purchase.

WAX OR NON WAX: WHICH TO CHOOSE

To decide which sort to buy you have to guess how much skiing you are going to do and where you are going to do it. It is safe to suggest fibreglass over wood, but then it depends how much opportunity you are going to get to actually ski, although remember that providing you have got the snow, you can cross country ski almost anywhere — the local park, along a footpath, even round the garden. However, if you are an occasional weekend or holiday ski tourer, then I would recommend a mohair, mica, or step-cut non-wax ski. Waxing is a technique where the ability grows with experience. If you only ski occasionally you will learn little and forget a lot, so a non-wax ski might be less trouble. However, you should still learn about waxes, for even step-cut skis work better with it.

My advice is to consider the following points:-

If you can tour regularly, or on a day only basis, and in the same area, then consider wax skis. The range of snow conditions, and variation in the weather will only cover a limited range which you will quickly learn to cope with.

My experience is that people who ski a lot in one area have a decided preference for waxing, be they in Western Canada, Southern France or Norway. However, the waxes in question vary considerably, and each disagrees with the others on points of technique.

I travel about to ski and have had to arrive at a system which copes with most conditions, so I use general touring or mountain non-wax skis, BUT with running waxes on tip and tail. It's a compromise, but it suits me. I am allowing for the widest possible changes in snow and terrain, and if I sacrifice a little performance in the process I am spared much aggravation.

On long tours wax skis are a problem. The snow state changes from day to day and place to place, so the waxing tourer has to carry a range of waxes and change them often. Many skiers enjoy this, but it certainly isn't necessary.

So my advice to the ski tourer is to go for general touring non-wax steel edged skis, of between 54mm and 58mm width at the waist, with three pin bindings — and I practise what I preach.

BUYING SKIS

Let us now consider the features you should look for when buying or hiring skis.

LENGTH

Cross country skis are long. The best guide is to hold the hand up over the head, and take a ski which comes up to the wrist. Beginners hiring skis

SOFT CAMBER: NO ARCH WHEN SKIS ARE WEIGHTED.

STIFF CAMBER: SOME CAMBER WHEN SKIS ARE EQUALLY WEIGHTED
NO CAMBER WHEN ONE SKI BEARS ALL THE WEIGHT.

might prefer skis a little shorter, while if you are tall or heavy, then perhaps one a little longer would be better, but the length is only part of it.

CAMBER AND FLEXIBILITY

Cross country skis, if held together base to base, exhibit a considerable curve or 'camber'. Grasp the skis between fingers and thumb in the high arch at the waist and squeeze them together. Check that they lie flat together all along their length, as any failure to do so indicates distortion.

Camber is the amount of arc or curve in the skis. The amount of resistance to flattening is called 'flex'. When gliding your weight must be spread evenly along the entire length, and it is the 'camber' which does this and thereby assists the 'kick' and 'glide' phases. Racing skis have a stiff camber and are hard to flex, while mountain skis are relatively soft.

The skis should come together firmly, but without undue difficulty. If they snap together the skis are too soft, too flexible, and the tips and tails may rise when your weight goes on them. If they are virtually impossible to squeeze together, they are too stiff, and you may not rest evenly on the snow. So, as a first step, you want skis which you can squeeze together with some little effort.

Try another test. Lay the skis down on a hard even floor (not a carpet) and stand on them at the waist, with a thin piece of paper underneath, weight evenly on both skis. Have the assistant try to slip the piece of paper out from under them. The piece of paper should slip out easily. If it won't the skis are too soft for your weight. If on the other hand you can get a wedge of carboard out, then they are too stiff. The ski tourer should try this test wearing his loaded rucksack. An extra 10-15lb. will not make much difference but 30lb. certainly will and could flatten out the camber completely, thus eliminating glide. On the other hand I have seen teenagers on very stiff skis unable to get along because they were too light to flatten the skis for the kicking stage. Do not neglect to try the finger and paper tests and insist that the assistant carries them out.

WAIST

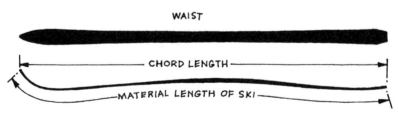

CHORD LENGTH

MATERIAL LENGTH OF SKI

HIRE

You do not have to buy, for you can usually hire, even in downhill resorts nowadays, and in the beginning, until you are certain that you like cross country skiing and have decided which type, and how much you will be able to do, hiring is far the best way to learn what suits you best.

However, if you do buy, I would recommend general touring equipment, choosing fibreglass skis, with serious consideration to a non-wax type. Think it over, read the books and journals, talk to the sales assistant, and while you are at it invest in a few bits and pieces.

SPARE SKI TIP

This is a hollow replica, in metal or plastic, of a ski tip. It is not difficult to break a ski in the woods and if it shears off when you are in the wilds you will have trouble getting home. The spare tip clips on to the body of the ski and is secured there with screws or a serrated clamp, and will get you home.

POLE BASKET

It is quite easy also to wrench the basket off the pole, having caught it under some tree root. Skiing without a basket is a lopsided affair, so buy a spare and put it in the sac. A plastic basket weighs next to nothing and is easily stowed away.

REPAIR OUTFIT

You should carry, perhaps on a group basis, a spare binding, some epoxy resin and a 'pozi'-drive or small screwdriver. A pair of needle-point pliers can be useful.

It is very easy to get over complicated when discussing XC equipment. There are over 200 different models available in skis alone, and when you add questions of bindings, surfaces, waxes or non-waxes, the combinations are almost infinite. The ski tourer requires a range of equipment which will convey him or her safely through the wilderness, and stand up to rough conditions, treatment and terrain. If you choose equipment which can do this your task will be easier and your enjoyment enhanced.

5 · Snow and Ski Waxes

Let us start with snow. The cross country skier has to be far more concerned with the state of the snow than the downhill alpine skier. The downhill skier usually skis on a prepared 'piste', regularly serviced by snow-cats or amtracks and, on or off piste, his heavier steel-edged skis ride over or through ruts and ice which would disconcert the cross country ski-tourer who uses lighter equipment and who usually travels off-piste anyway.

Many popular places do have prepared touring trails or *loipe* for the use of the cross-country skier, running over the hills and through the woods. Some even get provided with 'tramlines' to take the skis, but even here, because of variation in terrain and the presence of trees, sun and shade, the snow surface can change. However, these trails are an excellent place to learn about snow, waxing and XC technique.

If you used waxed skis, the changes in terrain and snow surface will affect the performance of the wax, and an understanding of snow for this purpose alone is useful. It is also essential for the understanding of avalanche conditions and to make estimates of time and distance on longer back-country tours.

FALLING SNOW
Snowflakes are composed of crystals. One estimate has it that there are some 6000 different kinds of snowflake, and air temperture decides the form they take while falling. If it is warm, the crystals can form up into large wet flakes. If it is very cold, you can get the little soft pellets, or 'granules', which are caused by the flakes falling through surface fog or cloud. The state of falling snow can change even as it falls so that wet (over 0°C) and dry (under 0°C) snow, can be contained in the same snowfall.

Broadly speaking, snow may be defined as 'wet' or 'dry' but this in turn can vary from 'very dry' which is very light snow which can be kicked up or swirled about like dust, to the heavy clinging type, which melts to soak through your clothes and will form a heavy snowball or a lump of ice if squeezed in the hand.

METAMORPHISM
As soon as a snowflake lands it starts to change, and this initial change is just one of a continuing series collectively referred to as *Metamorphism.* The first noticeable effect of this is that a fall of fresh snow, often high and fluffy, will settle into a more even and cohesive mass within a few days. This is caused by the melting and fusing together of the original snow crystals. The powder snow so beloved of skiers usually develops up to three days *after a fall.* Throughout the winter, as snow fall follows snow fall, each fall has different characteristics because of the varying conditions. The temperature within each layer and the consistency of the

snow itself will vary. Snow collects and the lower layers, under pressure from above, are continually melting. Water vapour from below is extracted by pressure and extruded into the upper layers. The lower crystals are continually fusing together and changing shape. This process is referred to scientifically as *constructive metamorphism.* The crystals eventually form what is referred to as cup-crystals. These are quite large, up to half an inch long, and naturally, cup-shaped.

This is a sketchy outline, but you can, I hope, see a pattern of light snowflakes on the top, increasing as the depth increases to larger ice crystals at the bottom. These varying shapes are continually changing, but the layers do not mis. It is as if fine sand was layered on top of gravel, which in turn rested on large pebbles. This mass is inherently unstable.

The next stage, often found in early spring, is produced by the continual melting and refreezing of the surface snow, which produces a coarse or 'corn' snow, often encountered on the sunny side of mountains. It is the quality of the surface layer which affects ski and wax performance.

POWDER
Snow is both viscous and compactable. Being viscous it will flow or creep, always taking the line of least restriction. Being compactable it will compress, and melt in the process. A skier's weight will compress the snow and the friction of the ski melts the crystals and permits glide.

Powder snow is dry and found below freezing point, and is said to be the skier's delight. It can be a pest to the tourer for it will infiltrate the clothing and melt, and it is impossible to keep out of a tent. In powder you may *need* wide long skis, but true powder is rare, so just relax, enjoy it and if you fall in powder, well, you won't hurt yourself.

WIND AND SNOW
Wind affects snow. Warm winds will melt it and then it freezes again. Wind blows the snow about, forming deep drifts. Wind shapes the heavier snow and forms ridges and cornices on the edge of escarpments. Wind pressure and the movement thus created over the snow can melt the snow crystals, but they later refreeze into hard *windslab* and stepped snow faces. Drifted snow under trees or in the lee of rocks can be of quite different composition from the snow all about it, and is often deep and soft. Snow varies — remember that.

SKARE
Hard, icy snow, rutted by wind or ski tracks, is often referred to as 'skare'. It is hard stuff to ski on, to the point where it is often as well to walk. A knowledge of snow is the basis of snow craft, one of the fundamental skills needed by cross country skiers, and ski tourers. Once you understand snow, you can make sensible waxing decisions, and be much safer in the wild.

THE GLOVE TEST
Most cross country skiers prefer to check the temperature by the state of the snow, rather than by using a thermometer, which just records the air temperature. Cross country skiers use the 'glove test'.

You pick up a handful of snow in your gloved hand and squeeze it. Open your hand and see what has happened.

1. A snowball has formed, or moisture on the glove = WET SNOW = Above Zero°.
2. If the snow blows away = DRY SNOW = Below Zero°.
3. If the snowball crumbles and can be blown = TRANSITIONAL SNOW = About Zero°.

It may seem crude, but for the touring skier it is quite adequate, and this information is your first guide to the correct wax.

WAXING
Nothing pre-occupies the cross country skier so much as waxes and waxing. The subject offers endless opportunities for discussion and argument, expertise and error. To the experienced skier all this debate is great fun, but to the beginner it is confusing and can be a little worrying, so let us start by assuring the beginner that there is very little to worry about. A few simple rules and guidelines will quickly overcome most of the problems you may encounter, and if it is still too much there are simple waxing methods or you need not wax at all.

HOW WAX WORKS
Until quite recently, when step-cut and mica-soled skis were introduced, all XC skis had to be waxed for efficient performance. Waxing is an art and a correctly waxed ski not only enables the ski to slide over the surface, but also the same wax will give sufficient grip for an uphill climb. This may sound incredible, but the principle is simple. The correct wax allows the snow crystals to bite in for 'grip' when the ski is firmly placed on the snow. At the same time, when the ski is put in motion and slid forward, pressure and friction melts the snow and a lubricating layer of water between wax and snow permits the ski to 'glide' forward.

The right balance between 'grip' and 'glide' is the aim of the XC skier.

As a ski-tourer I have largely but not entirely abandoned waxing in favour of the non-wax ski. This is less efficient but, and I stress that this is a personal opinion, I accept some loss in performance in return for fewer worries over waxing. Nevertheless, all XC skiers should know at least something about waxes and waxing for even the non-wax ski works better with a little wax.

TYPES OF WAX
One of the problems with learning about waxes is the problem of terminology. I have consulted two eminent authorities and read the standard works on the subject, and ended up confused because the words and terms employed lack definition, and are frequently mixed up. I will try here to be simple and precise, but beware of waxing words — they can mislead you.

The three basic categories of 'wax' are tars, base waxes (sometimes called sealer waxes, or, on PT bases, glider waxes) and running waxes (sometimes called 'kicker' or 'climbing' waxes).

Running (or kicker) waxes are then broken down, broadly, into hard waxes, and klisters.

Hard waxes come in little cans, klisters in tubes. Broadly speaking, the harder and newer the snow, the harder the wax. Klisters are generally used when the temperature is above 32°F (0°C) or on crust.

THE USES OF WAX
If we stick to our three basic categories, the uses are as follows:

TARS
Tars, which now come in spray-cans are used for sealing the bases of wooden skis. Without this protection water will enter the wood, freeze, and

gradually open up the base until it splits. Running waxes can be applied directly to the tars, or you *can* put on a base wax.

BASE WAXES (Sealers)
The prime purpose of a base wax is to help a running wax stick to the ski. Opinions vary as to whether they are necessary on synthetic bases, but I think they are. Base waxes are also now available in aerosol form.

RUNNING WAXES (Kick & Glide)
I am talking now about waxing for *touring,* not for racing. Racing skis have a high camber and except for a moment in the hard kick phase, the waists have little contact with the snow and this calls for precise waxing. The tourer, especially if carrying a heavy pack, has his skis well planted in the snow and should wax the entire ski. The ski base may conveniently be divided into three sections, tip, centre and tail, each section being about 2 feet long.

Glide, or running waxes go on the tip and tail, kicker waxes in the centre, for grip. The type of wax used depends on the conditions, but you would use a softer wax in the centre, for extra grip, if necessary. It may not in fact be necessary, and you could use one wax for the entire length of the ski, but if you slip going up slopes then, among other things, a softer wax in the centre section may help you. If you have too much grip, then cork the wax out, but more of this later. 'Klister' waxes are sticky and used for grip, so these should go in the centre section only.

How much time you spend waxing depends initially on your skis. These fall into three main types.

1. *Wooden skis:* Wooden skis need the full waxing treatment. The raw wood base must be sealed with tar against wet, otherwise water will enter the wood, freeze into ice and crack the ski. This tar can be melted on, painted on or comes in spray-cans and serves as a 'base' for the full range of running waxes.

2. *Skis with synthetic running surfaces:* Most racing skis have synthetic bottoms of polyethylene (P-Tex) of medium density for touring. These skis need no base waxes and only running waxes, although some manufacturers recommend a full base treatment of parrafin wax at the start of the season. These skis will slip anyway, so you usually wax for 'grip' rather than glide but they still need glide waxes, at tip and tail.

3. *Non-wax skis:* In theory no waxing is required, certainly not on mica-based skis. I have, however, two pairs of step-cut skis and while they are fine for climbing and very effective on the flat, I find them slow downhill, and therefore use a little 'glide' wax on the tips, well forward, and on the tails, which helps the glide considerably.

BASIC WAXING RULES
A first point is that the colder and newer the snow, the harder the wax. Klisters are for old, crusty snow, and in wet 'above zero' temperatures. One basic point is that for the proper application of wax your skis must be clean and dry. Keep them in a ski-bag for transportation or when not in use, as the wax will not stick to wet or gritty surfaces. Clean off the old wax with solvent, and start with a clean dry ski.

If you keep to the following rules most of your waxing problems will be fairly minor, although waxing is an art and calls for both judgement and experience.

1. Stick to one brand of wax.
2. Read the instructions on the can or tube before application and obey them.
3. Remember: A soft wax gives more grip than a hard wax, but less glide.
4. Remember: You can put a soft wax on a hard wax but not vice-versa, except in the case of 'cushion' waxing of which more later.
5. Wax neatly, for making a good job of the waxing improves the performance.
6. Remember: Several *thin* layers give more grip than one *thick* one.
7. If you have too much 'grip' try rubbing the wax out thinner and smoother with a cork. If you have too little, then rough on a little more, but don't smooth it out.
8. Remember: Freezing point is 0°C or 32°F. Above 0°C the snow is *'wet'* — below 0°C the snow is *dry*. About 0°C or 32°F the snow is transitional.
9. Learn to judge the snow by feel or by the 'glove test'. See page
10. Apply the wax to dry skis, for it won't go on otherwise.

Now since that may seem a lot of rules, let us just go into the reasoning behind them:-

1. Most manufacturers code waxes by colour but each manufacturer uses a slightly different range of colours. Stick to one brand and you will know where you are.
2. For the same reason read the use and application instructions on the wax can or tube. One man's 'Klister' is another man's sticking point. This also avoids the necessity to have a memory like an elephant.
3-4. If you put a hard wax on top of a soft wax it will just cut through — because it's harder! You will have to scrape the soft wax off to apply the hard wax — so, if in doubt use a harder wax first. An exception to this is 'cushion' waxing, chipping hard wax on top of frozen klister. This is used on transitional days when you start on mushy snow on a route across frozen snow in the woods.
5-6. A neat job gives better results. Read the application instructions and 'cork' the wax out properly. A good corking improves a good waxing. You can often thin the wax out by rubbing it down with a cork and so get more glide, without having to scrape the lot off and start again.

APPLYING THE WAX.

SMOOTHING WAX WITH A CORK.

47

8-9. The basic decision is between *wet* and *dry* snow, but the permutations are endless. Don't try and remember them. Use your chosen manufacturer's waxing chart.

10. This is why you are recommended to buy a ski bag for transportation. You are better off waxing indoors, but the skis, once waxed, must be put outside to adjust to the temperature before you start to ski.

WAXING KIT
The basic kit consists of just four items:-
1. Some hard waxes and klisters.
2. A waxing cork.
3. A scraper.
4. A solvent for removing wax, especially Klisters. *Klister* is a Norse word which means 'sticky' — and it is!

Buy a plastic bag to keep them in, as loose waxes can make a mess. As time goes on and you become more experienced, you may also want:-
1. A waxing iron — used for melting and spreading wax on skis. Any old iron will do, or you can use:-
2. A waxing torch — this is a mini-blowtorch used for putting on base wax, sometimes for removing old wax instead of a solvent, and warming the waxing iron. Use it with care or you will scorch the skis.

Fortunately these latter items are being rapidly superseded by the introduction of aerosol or spray-can solvents and waxes which are a boon to the ski-tourer.

RUNNING WAXES AND KLISTERS
Each major manufacturer at present has a range of about a dozen 'running' waxes and 'klisters'.

Running waxes: These come in little colour-coded cans, and are, broadly speaking, used on new, dry, or powder snow. Most manufacturers code in Green, Blue, Violet or Red, for this snow states.

Klisters: Klisters come in colour-coded tubes or increasingly in aerosol cans. Klister is used on older, slushy, or settled packed snow.

Between these extremes, on settled snow, the wax used very much depends on the temperature.

To this basic range we have to add for the non-wax ski that need more glide:-

Glider waxes: These are a conventional running wax usually paraffin based, and are used on synthetic bases, even on the tips and tails of non-wax skis — to increase glide. Apply the wax well forward on the tip, or it will gradually work back to the 'step cut' or 'fish tail' and reduce the grip. Put some in the ski groove and along the edges of the ski, even on the tops. It will help the snow slip off, and it all reduces drag. Aerosol glide waxes are very convenient and the ones by *Swix* are excellent.

HOW TO WAX
If you have wooden-soled skis you will have applied a protective tar and for the synthetic probably a base preparation, but from this point on the waxing drill is basically the same for all sorts of ski surfaces.

1. Check the snow. The type of wax and the method of application will depend on the snow state. Is it new or old, hard crust or powder, above or below freezing? The 'glove test' is a good simple guide and should always be used.
2. Select a wax, and READ THE INSTRUCTIONS on tube or can. On the trail keep some wax inside your sweater, where body heat will keep it pliant and easy to use.
3. Wax indoors if possible. Be sure the skis are clean, dry and free from grit and old wax.
4. Apply the running wax, covering the entire surface of the ski. The higher the temperature the rougher the surface of the wax finish should be, so apply the wax roughly initially. 'Kicker' waxes like Klisters need only be applied for up to a metre under the foot. In this case a 'kicker' wax is a softer wax, and gives more grip.
5. If, instead of more grip you need good glide, then cork the wax out smoothly.
6. Put the skis outside to adjust to the cold, and then *test your wax* by skiing around for a few minutes. If you have too much grip cork the wax out some more. If not enough grip, put on some more wax, in a rough surface. The right wax, or wax combination, correctly applied, gives both grip and glide.

KLISTERS

Klisters come in tubes, and to apply them successfully you need to warm up the tubes first and then apply the klister. Smooth out the klister with a spreader, not your hand. It's messy, but you can wipe your spreader clean with a little solvent. Don't put on too much klister. Put on small toothbrush size drops and smooth it out well. Put a thin layer on first, as removing klister is a difficult operation. Aerosol klisters are available, with attached spreader. You will also need some warmth, and solvent to get the stuff off. Klister is a gripping wax and need only be applied on the 'kicker' area, under the binding. Keep it out of the ski groove where you can apply a lick of glide wax.

BASE WAXES

Synthetic skis don't hold running waxes as well as tar-treated wood, and you *may* need to apply a base wax to the polyethylene to provide a binder for the running wax. You can obtain spray-on base wax preparations, or you can paint or melt base-wax on from a can. Most modern P.Tex bases do not require base waxing.

REMOVING THE WAX

The three common methods of removing waxes are:-
1. By scraper.
2. By melting it off with a blowtorch, although this risks damaging the ski.
3. By the use of solvents.

A scraper is a basic item, and which of the other two you use depends on their availability. Some aerosol wax solvents are made to be sprayed directly onto the ski, but it is better with others to dampen a soft rag and wipe it over the ski in order to remove the wax.

WAXING AREAS

Because I believe it is better I recommend that except for klister you wax the whole ski, but many authorities recommend that, with synthetic bases you need only wax the 'kicking' area, i.e., the part under the foot. Synthetic skis are designed with cambers suitable for glide waxing, at tip and tail and often have a marked scale in the 'kicking' wax area to help you remember how much of it you have covered. Many experienced ski tourers recommend using a paraffin glide wax in the ski groove, which can collect ice, rather than the running wax. The aim is the same, to ski cross-country with ease, and experience will teach you which method and which waxes work best for you in certain conditions. Follow the waxing instructions and the basic rules, or, a good idea for the ski-tourer, use 'wide range' waxes.

WIDE RANGE WAXES

The ski tourer can avoid much waxing toil and expense if, initially anyway, he sticks to using Universal or 'Wide-Range' waxes.

The basic idea of a 'wide-range' wax is that it cuts the waxing decisions down to one. Is the snow above or below freezing? Or, to put it another way, is the snow *wet* — (above 0°C) or *dry* — (below 0°C).

Wide-range wax manufacturers reduce the calculations still further by naming the waxes in a single fashion, and most major manufacturers now have a wide range wax. For example:

Snow	Temp.	Manufacturer		
		REX	SWIX	TOKO
Wet	Above 0°C	Plus	Plus	Plus
Dry	Below 0°C	Minus	Minus	Minus

It could hardly be easier!

GENERAL WAXES

Apart from not waxing at all, or using wide-range waxes, you can solve the problem by using simple charts.

FALLING OR NEW SNOW

Snow state	Manufacturer			
	TOKO	SWIX	REX	RODE
Fine flakes	Olive or green	Green	Green	Green
Dry flakes	Blue	Blue	Blue	Blue
Forms a snowball (Moist)	Red	Violet or Yellow	Violet or Yellow	Violet or Yellow
Leaves hand wet (Wet)	Yellow or red Klister	Yellow Klister	Red Klister	Red Klister

If the snow is a day or two old it has settled, so use this chart:-

SETTLED SNOW

Snow state	Manufacturer			
	TOKO	SWIX	REX	ROSE
Small grains	Green	Green	Green	Green
Large grains, Lumps	Blue or Violet	Blue	Blue or Violet Klister	Blue
Forms wet snowball	Yellow	Blue or Violet	Red or Red Klister	Violet
Leaves hands very wet	Red or Violet Klister	Red Klister	Red Klister	Red or Silver Klister

After a few days, with warm days and freezing nights, the snow's construction starts to break down; it has *metamorphised,* so you use this one:-

OLD (METAMORPHISED) SNOW

Snow state	Manufacturer			
	TOKO	SWIX	REX	RODE
Hard crust 'skare'	Blue Klister	Blue Klister	Blue	Red Klister
Crumbly, granulated	Violet Klister	Violet Klister	Violet Klister	Blue or Violet Klister
Melting wet	Red Klister	Red Klister	Silver or Red Klister	Silver of Black Klister

Please note that these charts leave out many variations, such as Light Greens, Special Blues etc. Where two colours appear in one box the second is the one to use when the snow may be wetter than you suppose or is clearly melting. New waxes are appearing all the time so obtain current waxing charts to keep fully up to date.

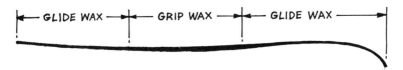

NON-WAX SKIS

I still find it necessary to put 'glide' wax on my 'non-wax' skis. Applied thinly it helps on the flat and downhill where otherwise the skis seem a little slow. I put the wax on the tail of the ski, from behind the 'cut', but well forward on the 'shovel' leaving a good gap so that it cannot work back into the 'cut' section. With mohair skis you don't have this problem but the mohair can ice up. A preparation called WD40 or any silicone spray will prevent this happening.

RUNNING IN

No wax will perform efficiently until it has been used for a little while, and has run in and adjusted to temperature. Don't expect much until you have covered, say, a quarter of a mile (.3km.) on skis.

ADVICE

The best piece of advice I have had on waxing was to use my eyes and if in doubt, ask. If you see someone motoring along with great ease, ask him how he is waxed. Store up such advice for future use and don't be too embarrassed to ask for it. Don't blame all grip and glide problems on your wax, or lack of it. Poor technique can multiply your problems in this area too.

The ski-tourer, on a day tour in his home area can wax, and will soon learn the waxes necessary for local condition. Ski-ing away from base, or over several days then, in my opinion, you are better off on non-wax skis, or using wide-range waxes, and those taking up ski-touring would be well advised to give these methods serious consideration, at least to begin with.

6 · Skiing Techniques

The basic movement in cross country skiing is the *Diagonal Stride*. This is essentially a loping striding slide, the arms swinging forward, shoulders high and back, weight always going forward on to the front ski and giving impetus to the stride.

Many skiers define the diagonal stride as an extension of the normal walking movement but it isn't as simple as that. It is, however, far from difficult, so to learn the knack I suggest you try the following:-

DIAGONAL STRIDE

Find a flat piece of snow, up to 50 metres long and fairly wide. Position yourself at one end, skis parallel and about 6″ (15cm.) apart. Now start to walk across the snow, left leg first, swinging the right arm shoulder high. Lift and place the pole just forward of the boot. Be sure the pole slants back from the wrist and is not prodded forward into the snow.

Continue, swinging the arms alternately, left leg — right arm, right arm — left leg. Make this a positive movement. Avoid weak swings which will end up with you swinging the right arm with the right leg. Swing the arms well to the rear. That extra swing back helps push you forward, and leans the body into the glide.

After about six or seven paces, when the arms are swinging well, lean forward, bend the knees and *kick* with the rear foot while sliding the first foot forward with your weight entirely on it. This should change your walk into a powerful forward skating movement, and you must take advantage of it and prolong the glide as far as possible. Your weight should be comfortably forward on the gliding forward ski. Balance can be a problem initially, but you will soon get used to it. While you slide, bring the rear foot up with alternate arm, plant pole, and kick again with the rear foot, and so continue. Kick, slide, arm swing, plant pole, kick! — and you're off!

Once you have the general idea, refine your technique. Keep the arms swinging and the knees bent. You can't kick with a straight leg. Keep going, don't stop kicking. Always ski, don't plod. You can 'kick and glide' quite slowly, but keep the movement going. Laden ski tourers used to ignore technique, being content to just get along, but good technique makes it easier, faster and more fun.

To begin with, you may find it easier if you practise without poles. They help maintain balance and provide push, but they are something extra to think about, so try a few circuits without poles first, to get the arms swinging properly. I find poles an inch or two shorter than the recommended armpit length are slightly easier to manage.

The diagonal stride is not dissimilar to a skating movement, but is conducted not with side push but directly fore and aft. Once you get the idea, which should be the first time, if you follow these instructions, you will start to cover the ground quickly and easily, with firm kicks and long *glides.* Don't just kick and slide forward in the same position, and do not let the front leg become locked forward. Having kicked, the rear foot should be completely unweighted but coming through to take the weight and glide, while the *other* leg kicks. Don't let the first kicking leg trail. You need continuous flowing strides.

POLE TECHNIQUE

Examine the diagram carefully. Note that the pole always slants directly to the rear. Don't stab it forward, or out to the side. The pole provides about twenty-five per cent of your impetus if it is applied to the REAR, so don't waste the movement. Remember also to keep the arms at shoulder height apart, swinging them close to the sides. Don't spread them wide as this again wastes effort, and this is why rucksacks should be without side pockets which will certainly impede arm movement to the rear.

If you grip the poles tightly and heave yourself forward by the arms you will tire yourself out very quickly. Grasp the poles lightly, letting your weight bear down on the wrist strap. Let the grip slacken until, as you near the end of the movement, the pole is grasped lightly between thumb and first finger, ready to swing forward again.

DOUBLE POLING

You can use this to gain speed while sliding in the descent, or for extra impetus when doing the diagonal stride.

Swing both arms forward together, placing the poles firmly and swinging through to the rear. It is pretty tiring, but it can be useful when striding. Save effort by taking two kick-and-glide strides between each pole thrust, and remember to use the weight of the body, not the strength of your arms to power the poles back and the body forward.

TURNING

Turning on skis always bothers the tyro, even when standing still. Stopped, on the flat, you can simply shuffle round, taking care not to let the ski tails or tips cross. This is not very graceful but it gets you there. On a slope you use the 'kick-turn', which is also useful, as illustrated here, for crossing low obstacles.

The secret of a successful kick turn is to plant the poles clear of the skis. The most simple rule is 'PLANT THE POLE TO THE REAR OF THE FIRST SKI YOU MOVE'. This will cover you for all eventualities, for you swing your first ski round the planted pole, transfer the weight onto it and then bring the other ski over.

SKATING OR 'STEP' TURNS

Next to the diagonal stride the skate or step turn is the most useful touring manoeuvre, and one you will need all the time. You use it for stopping a downhill schuss, or a traverse. A neat skate turn can get you out of rutted 'tramlines', past a fallen friend, or round a tree. So time spent learning and practising the step turn will not be wasted.

Let us run down a slope and make a step turn to the right. Start double poling and bend the knees. For the turn, first be sure you are running on parallel skis. Transfer all your weight on the *left* ski. Now lift the right unweighted one which is then pointed off 45° into the new direction, and kick off the left *weighted* ski, transferring the weight on to the right *gliding*

one. Bring the left ski parallel and off you go, 45° in the new direction. Now try it to the left. With a load on this is the best turn for stopping, and it may be that you will have to make several step (or skate) turns to get 90° to the slope and stop. Work on the skate (or step) turn. It is the ski tourer's friend.

STEM TURNS
It is important to remember that most cross country skis, up to the 'mountain' variety, have no metal edges. Therefore turns, and especially the stem turn, must be executed by sliding and transferring the weight, and not by 'carving' the turn, as you can with heavy, edged downhill skis.

The stem is used for turning downhill at the end of a traverse, unlike the step turn where you turn uphill.

The routine is as follows:

1. Run the traverse, skis apart, knees bent, weight evenly on both skis; turning point approaches; the weight must be fairly well on the heels.
2. Still keeping the knees bent, transfer *all* the weight to the downhill ski. Then:-
3. Stem, by pressing out the heel and so pushing out the rear of the *upper* ski, making a wide 'V' of the tips.
4. Keeping the upper ski flat on the snow, transfer the weight slowly on to it. Lean *out* as your body swings round and look downhill.
5. Once round, the weight is now on the outside (downhill) ski. Bring in the unweighted upper ski, spread the weight evenly and continue the traverse. Repeat the process for the next turn. Without fixed bindings you must keep your heels *down* on the ski heel popper. Your weight must be down on the ski, neither back nor forward.

'SKATE' OR 'STEP' TURN

TELEMARK TURN

The telemark turn is a beautiful movement and far from difficult. You have probably seen the Telemark position on television, for this is the position which ski jumpers adopt on landing. The knees are bent, the rear leg trails, the arms are held out wide. You can gather that the Telemark position looks and feels very stable. The turn itself needs some two hours hard work on the slope to perfect, but the effort is well worthwhile.

Find an even slope, preferably with light snow cover, and go to the top.

1. Start down on the fall line with the knees bent, and with the skis slightly ploughed.
2. Slide one ski well ahead of the other, until the binding of the forward ski is level with the tip of the rear ski. All your weight is now forward, the rear ski is trailing and unweighted.
3. Keep the poles out at right angles to aid stability.
4. Now stem the forward ski lightly and you will go round in a wide graceful turn. If your right leg is in front you stem it out and left, to turn to the right. Telemark round, and then repeat the manoeuvre to the left. Keep low.
5. Let the rear ski trail. Remember that the rear leg is bent. Below the knee your leg is parallel to the trailing ski.
6. Expect a few falls before you get the knack, for learning a telemark turn is rather like learning to ride a bicycle. Once you get the hang of it you don't fall off so much. Balance is critical and it is awkward with a heavy pack.

Linked Telemark turns are an excellent way of descending those wide, long, open slopes which are a mite too steep. You can build up a considerable speed on cross country skis, so if a slope appals you there is no disgrace in taking off the skis and walking.

STOPPING: SNOWPLOUGH STOP

Until you become very good you will probably rely on the snowplough position, both to slow down and stop you.

In the Snowplough the knees are bent, and the heels, well down on the heel plate, are forced out, the ski tips making a 'V'. Don't let speed build up before you do this. Ski tourers are cautious about descending slopes without a good clear run out at the bottom and must control their speed.

FALLING

Falling is often referred to as the 'second' method of stopping, and is quite legitimte. Slow down before you fall and fall uphill, where it is easier to regain your feet. If you have to fall do it before you are out of control. One fall to avoid is where your ski tips drift apart and you fall forward on to your face. This can easily pull knee ligaments and cause quite severe injury. If this appears likely, lift one ski up, cross it over the other, and go into a sideways roll. It won't be elegant, but you won't run much risk either.

SPEED CONTROL

If it is any consolation you are not usually going as fast as you seem to be. It just seems fast. There are various techniques to reduce speed, and the following should be practised and employed when necessary.

1. *Pole squatting:* Put the poles between the legs, and sit on them, hobby horse fashion. The baskets will dig into the snow and make a useful brake.
2. *One-on-one-off:* If you are running down a trail, have one ski off the loipe, either in the middle of the track or off to one side. The deeper untracked snow will slow you down.
3. *Stemming and side-stepping:* Running down an open slope, plant the pole forward, bending the knees and stem out, pressing out the heels. Let the resulting turn become wide. Just brake a little and stem from side to side, Use any hump and side-slip off it to lose speed. If the slope is too steep, too narrow, or too icy, take off the skis and walk.

Now let's talk about climbing:-

CLIMBING — Diagonal Stride
The diagonal stride will get you up most reasonable slopes if you remember to keep the weight forward, and the knees bent. Don't try for a long glide on the uphill. Short, even strides will get you there quicker together with short thrusts from the poles. The crucial thing is to keep the weight forward and move on your toes, planting the ski firmly to let the wax or step-cut bite.

RUNNING STRIDE
A shorter but steeper slope can be overcome by taking it at a run. Bound forward, throwing the weight from the rear to front ski, and your impetus will probably get you there. On some snow it feels like a trampoline. If this doesn't work you still have three remaining choices.

SIDE STEPPING
Start at the bottom, skis at right angles to the fall line, weight on lower ski. Lift the upper ski to the uphill side, about 12 inches. Transfer the weight on to it. Now bring up the lower leg. Repeat, until you get to the top. It is very important to keep the skis parallel to the fall line or you can slide away, either forward or back.

HERRINGBONE
The Herringbone takes its name from the pattern the skis leave behind on the fresh snow.
Facing the slope, point the skis out sideways, heels together in the reverse of the snowplough position. Keep the knees bent in together and climb the slope, gripping with the inside edges of the skis. The herringbone is much faster, but more tiring than the side step, but is useful for short steep slopes.

TRAVERSE TURNS
Big wide slopes lend themselves to the traverse turn. Take the slope at an angle, and zig-zagging your way up, use the alternative stride, single poled, for the traverse, and an uphill skating — or if the slope is steep — kick-turn for the corners. You will need to edge the skis for the turns, and if the slope is very steep or icy, use the kick-turn, turning across your own uphill tracks at about 45°, to start the new traverse.

SIDE STEPPING

HERRINGBONE CLIMBING

59

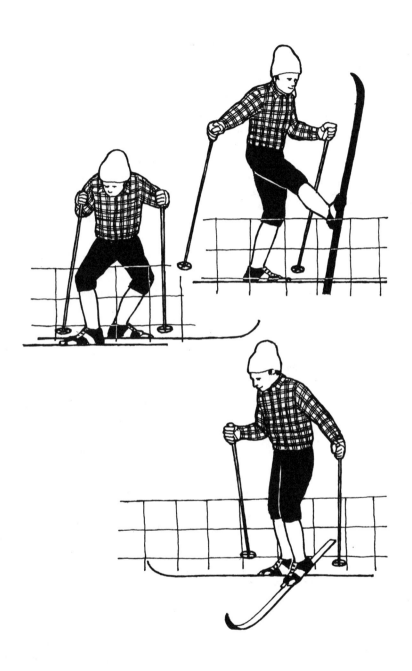

COMING DOWN

SCHUSS

The easiest way of descent is the straight, skis parallel, downhill 'schuss'. Stay upright, weight evenly on both feet and down on the heels. Now let yourself go. Keep the knees bent and hold the poles out at right angles to the body. This can help you to maintain balance while crossing bumps, but above all keep the weight *down* on the heels. You have no fixed heel binding remember, so the weight is your security.

TREES

If your path takes you down through trees or bushes, remove the hands from the pole loops for if the basket catches on a branch or foot, you may drop the pole, but if your wrist is wound in the strap you will get a badly wrenched arm as well. This has happened to me and it is *not* just a theory.

TRAVERSING

Unless the slope is shallow, or has a good run out, or another slope to climb on the far side, the downhill schuss, especially with a loaded rucksack on your back, is a trifle risky. These situations do in fact happen quite often, but when in doubt, *traverse,* running across the slope with the skis edged and the knees bent into the hill.

Run down the slope, at an angle, criss-crossing it at the end of each traverse, and side slipping on the run both to lose height and slow down.

SIDE SLIPPING

To side slip, run at a little less than right angles across the fall line, and on any hump or even slope, let the skis flatten on the snow and swing the hips and knees gently out. The skis will slide under you down the slope. To stop the side slip move your weight forward and turn the ski tips down the slope.

OBSTACLES

Inevitably when touring you will meet obstacles. By its very nature cross country skiing takes the skier up to natural or man-made obstacles. Since it is not always possible to remove the skis to cross them, the cross country skier has evolved ways of doing so while keeping the skis on. Snow has often drifted deeply against walls and fences, so you must keep your skis on to avoid sinking up to your waist or deeper. Cross country equipment is mercifully light, so that given a little agility you will soon be able to perform these simple manoeuvres without difficulty.

LOW WALLS

Stand parallel with the wall, and if it is snow covered, step up on to it. Now bring up the other leg, then one ski down, then the other. If the drop is greater on the other side, put the poles down for stability and jump off, feet together. Beware of this with a loaded pack. Never jump *off* anything you can't jump *on*. Take the pack off first.

BACK ROLLS

If the wall is wide or up to waist high, try rolling over it on your back. Sit or lean back on the wall. Lie down on the top, lifting the skis, and roll over sideways to put the feet down flat on the far side.

FENCE JUMP

For obstacles up to waist height, try jumping. This can't be done with a pack on, so put the pack over first. Find a fence-post and stand parallel with the fence. Remove the hands from the pole straps and place the poles close to the outer ski. Place the other hand on the fence post, and swing between post and poles. Take a breath and:-

1. Swing up, bending the knees to raise the skis.
2. Jump around, twisting over the fence.
3. Land on both skis on the far side facing the other way.

As with the Telemark, it's a knack, and needs a little practice. An obstacle crossing 'follow-my-leader' game, played to and fro over a fence, is the best way to learn this very useful touring skill.

STREAMS

Be wary of streams. Quite apart from the obvious risks of drowning or wet feet — a problem in winter — don't splash across with your skis on, or they will ice up fast when you reach the snow. Try and find a snow bridge to cross by, but only if it is not too wide or the stream not too deep. Use fallen trees, or go higher up until the stream narrows. Better still use proper bridges — that's what they are there for. In the back country, cross streams and snow bridges one at a time and if you have a rope, rope up.

ROADS

Don't forget to check if anything is coming before you cross. Step on to the road, and lift the feet high when crossing. Do not slither or you will scrape the wax off, or damage the surface of your non-wax ski.

CONCLUSION

XC techniques, put simply, are not difficult. You can learn them adequately in a day. To learn them well, and ski with good polished technique and little effort is more difficult, but well worthwhile. Keep improving your technique for good techniques will spare you a great deal of effort.

7 · Ski Touring

GOOD BEGINNINGS

We are now more than half way through this book so let us just stop for a moment and review the steps we have covered so far.

1. We started with the promise that you, the reader, is already relatively experienced out-of-doors, and has a good grasp of basic outdoor skills before deciding to learn XC skiing and try ski touring.
2. We have described, and you have bought, hired or borrowed any necessary and suitable clothing, equipment and, of course, skis, boots and poles.
3. You have spent up to a week learning and perfecting the necessary XC techniques. This, plus the correct equipment and basic outdoor experience is the very minimum necessary before you embark on a tour.

Have you completed these three stages? If so, we can start going on tours out into the winter wilderness.

DAY TOURS

It is sensible to start ski touring on a day or even half-day basis, rather like starting walking or camping when you begin with short hikes or overnight pitches near home, before you go off for a week or more. If longer trips are your ambition, then day touring acts as a shake-down. I remember my very first trip on XC skis was a far too long 20-mile stint over the hills of the Auvergne. The last two miles is still my worst outdoor experience, and back at the hut I crawled into my bunk and stayed there, absolutely beat until the next morning. Even then, getting my stiff legs to function again was memorable. Biting off more than you can chew is common in all activities, but it is best avoided if possible.

SHORT TOURS

A short ski tour can last up to a day and eventually lead on to an overnight stop in a refuge, tent or snow-hole. Initially, I think you should plan a circular day or half-day tour, returning to base at the finish. The objects of day touring in this context are to improve your off-loipe ability, test clothing, equipment and technique, and generally prepare the skier for longer tours. Even though you are intending to operate for a shorter period the principles of touring remain the same, and so a series of day tours, if correctly planned and executed, is the ideal, indeed the only basis for the correct fulfilment of longer trips.

PLANNING

Many day tours can be made over prepared *loipe*. These trails often cover the route of summer footpaths and in North America, for example, are marked out in winter by sno-mobiles. If you are familiar with the area in summer you will have a good idea of the winter terrain and can make some sound decisions on time and distance. When planning my winter tours I like to go to places I have visited in summer.

Detailed planning is the basis of good touring, so, lacking a reconnaissance, get out the maps and study the terrain. Note particularly the height, the way the slopes face, and get an idea of snow cover.

A circular or loop tour can be fun and avoids the problem of getting back to your transport at the finish. It is sometimes possible to tour cross country between two points linked by rail or bus, or leave a car at either end of the lateral route, but be sure the transport runs in winter and at weekends.

Whichever you choose, be certain that you can get home again, and aim to finish the trip in good time. The use of pre-planning, even if the plan goes wrong, ensures that you get a good idea of your capabilities and the points which need to be checked. Besides, it's fun.

NUMBERS

The minimum in the party is really three and four would be better. Then in the event of trouble, you have spare people to send for help. On a day tour anyway it is not too important to have people of equal skiing ability. These trips are the time to improve and NOTHING IMPROVES SKIING LIKE THE TIME SPENT ON SKIS.

Choose terrain which gives an opportunity for all types of skiing, up, down and level, and work in some obstacle crossing. Before you go, try and pick places from the map for lunch stops. Work out escape routes off the hill in the event of bad weather, and prepare a route card, with map references, bearings and timings. Have this route card checked by other members in the party and leave a copy behind with some responsible person. Remember you are testing your techniques with a view to the future, so carry out the full routine. It will pay dividends later.

EQUIPMENT

Apart from normal XC clothing, skis, boots, poles and waxes, the day touring party needs the following items, contained in a light rucksack.

1. Spare warm clothing (especially socks).
2. Compass and map (can you use them?) (g)
3. Route card (g)
4. Ski tip, wire, pliers and screws, epoxy resin (g).
5. First aid kit (g)
6. Warm food in vacuum flask and/or: (g)
7. Food (plus stove) (g)
8. Whistle
9. Bivvy bag
10. Matches
11. Candle.
12. Waxes (g)

Items marked (g) can be carried on a group basis.

These should be taken on every tour. If you are going on a full day tour, each member should take a sleeping bag as well and the group should take:

1. A tent, and/or:-   2. A shovel.

VANGO FORCE 10

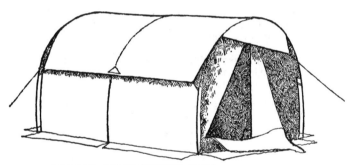

BLACKS NYLON TUNNEL TENT

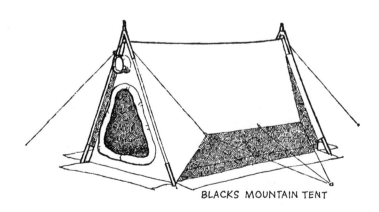

BLACKS MOUNTAIN TENT

If you are going out for half a day, it may extend to a whole day. If going for a day you *could* get stuck out overnight. And it's winter! If you have any walking in mind, consider ice axes as well. These last items may seem a pure frill, and if you are simply touring around a crowded resort loipe with plenty of skiers about, this may be true. However, even if they are not strictly necessary, it is good practice for later, longer tours. Besides, if it is snowing at lunch time you might even prefer to whack the tent up, or shovel out a windbreak, rather than just huddle under a tree. The real reason is safety and while I don't want to go on and on about danger, to the extent that ski touring sounds perilous, neither do I want to hear of someone found frozen to death with this book in his pocket. Remember:

Spring seduces
Summer thrills;
Autumn lulls
But Winter kills.

DISTANCES AND NAISMITHS RULE

The distance you can cover will depend on the weather, your skill, the snow state, and the terrain. Winter days, especially in the far north, can be very short, and overcast skies can make them even shorter. So, firstly, consult the map. Examine the hills, the forest, the streams, and imagine them under snow.

Mountaineers and hill walkers often use *'Naismiths Rule'* for calculating time and distance, and in my experience this works very well for XC touring as well. Naismiths Rule states that you should:-

"Estimate one hour for every three miles, plus one hour for every 2,000 feet climbed" — or descended.

This is an unladen estimate. If you are carrying heavy packs, these timings must be extended, and even though you get along faster on skis than you would walking, other factors, notably weather and short days, make a Naismiths estimate for a day a very reasonable one.

The terrain will govern your speed considerably. Over open rolling snowfields you can zip along at a great rate, but if the terrain is broken, with walls and fences, through woods, across heath or over rutted icy snow, your speed will be cut drastically. Initially I recommend you should restrict your day tours to four hours of travel and extend them as your skill and experience increases. You should be able to cover about 12 miles and that is a good start.

DAY TOURING ROUTINE

Start your tour the night before by listening to the weather forecast, checking your maps and route cards and going to bed early.

Check all your gear, and leave it in one place, where nothing can be overlooked in the morning. If travelling to the start by car check gear into the car so that nothing is left behind. An early start Is essential, so rise before dawn, and get away as soon as possible. This is the best time of the day, while the snow is unmarked, and the trails are empty. Start with a good breakfast and visit the lavatory. Both actions save discomfort later on.

You will, if using wax models, have waxed your skis before leaving, but don't expect your waxes to function well at first. You may have to travel a mile or more before you feel the stride coming through properly, and remember that the snow state will change throughout the day.

Try and strike a fast, but even pace, and if off-loipe, take it in turns to break trail and map read, tread out the path and choose the route. It's all good practice and these techniques and this work should be learned and shared.

After about an hour make a brief stop for adjustments. It is almost certain that everyone would like to tighten a lace, take off a sweater or change a wax, but all too often these minor adjustments could be neglected because no one wants to cry "Halt". Make it a group rule to have such a stop and solve a problem before it starts.

HALTS

Once you stop in winter you will start to chill down and it makes good sense and good practice to scan the country ahead for suitable halfway places, or even try and note them from the map. Ideally these should be sunny, in shallow snow, and out of the wind. Do not stop half way up a slope. It is far better to stop just below the crest out of the wind, or better still, once you have crossed it. Do not halt on avalanche slopes or below cornices, on ice or under snow-shedding trees. Trying to brew up under a wet snowfall is depressing. A dollop of snow will assuredly fall off the tree and land on the cooker at the crucial moment. Don't melt snow, it takes too long. Melt ice.

Avoid chilling down during the halt. I carry my windproofs strapped across the top of my pack and put them on as soon as I stop. This allows body heat and sweat to disperse slowly without that horrid feeling of wet chilly perspiration congealing on the body. Ugh!

FOOD

A warm meal is especially enjoyable in the winter. Dry or cold food is just as beneficial in calorific value, but the sensation is not the same. You will use up a lot of calories in the course of a day's ski tour, and should aim to consume about 4000 just to keep yourself going, avoid over-tiring and produce body heat.

Brewing up in the winter can be a slow business and where possible you should take hot food with you in vacuum flasks. Hot soups or stews can be kept warm easily, but the flasks need to be protected against breakage. Wrap them well, inside your spare clothing and when (not if) you fall, try not to fall on your pack. Put the flasks inside a sealed plastic bag just in case. Instead of taking tea or coffee, take hot water. This, mixed with a tea or coffee bags will give a better brew than if the full drink stews in the flask for several hours — and of course gives you a choice. Hot water can also be used to reconstitute AFD food and, all in all, is a useful winter 'store'.

Oranges, eaten with a lump of sugar will quench the thirst and give you a useful energy boost, while a steady consumption of chocolate, nuts or 'gorp' will keep the energy going. Nibble away, and keep the energy going.

While this is all you will need while day touring, it is good practice to cook at least one dish, on a stove, out in the snowfields, with a view to preparing all your meals out there, in the course of longer tours. With each such activity there are tips and wrinkles to be learned and these early tours are the place to learn them.

You can take fresh food with you, or some packed or freeze dried meals.

Read the instructions on such foods carefully, and examine them for cooking times and complications. You may find some difficulty in igniting a stove at low temperatures, and you will quickly discover that food in winter cooks quicker and stays warmer if your pots have lids. Plastic mugs and plates are warmer, lighter and less likely to burn the lips than metal, and as such are to be preferred.

Finally, once you have eaten, scatter any spare food scraps for the animals and birds, but clear up any non-biodegradable mess. If you bury tins and packets beneath the snow, out of sight may be out of mind, but they will reappear, a soggy, rusting mess in the Spring. The rule remains: If you pack it in — pack it out.

MAP AND COMPASS

Even when following a waymarked trail, use your map and compass, and always know where you are. There are those who think the map is more useful than the compass in winter, which amazes me. The winter landscape is so different from the summer one, and visibility can be so restricted and change so quickly that you can often only maintain your direction with a compass bearing. Make it a rule to take bearings on any landmark at regular intervals. Then if the visibility does close in you will be glad of any clues to where you are. The knowledge and use of backbearings is especially useful. You can easily retrace your steps by following your ski tracks, but if it starts to snow, or a 'white-out' develops, the tracks are soon lost.

TOURING TIPS

On a day touring level XC skiing is not so different from a summer hike. The rules are the same, although the results of breaking them can be more drastic, so here with a few tips;

STAY TOGETHER

There is no point in making up a party at all if one or more of the members range out on their own. This is one reason for trying to balance the party, but in any case the good or super fit member must not career off alone and leave the others behind. Selfish behaviour like this can ruin a tour and even be dangerous, especially to the Lone Ranger. They can get lost, choose a different route, or not be missed should they have an accident. At the very best, leaving the party will cause confusion and resentment and is sheer bad manners. My experience is that Lone Rangers inevitably cause more trouble than they are worth.

STAY ALERT

When skiing, keep the head up and look about you. Quite apart from enjoying the scenery and the exercise, you will be better fixed to observe changes in terrain and weather. Turnings need to be watched, and the decision to alter plans, if necessary, should be taken before the necessity arises.

TURNING BACK

Never worry about altering your plans or turning back. It's supposed to be fun. Remember you must advise anyone anticipating your return or arrival what you have done, or you may start an unnecessary search. If you get into trouble, find the chosen route too difficult, or the weather conditions are just misery, then don't battle on blindly, but at the same time always give it a go before you finally give up. Experience comes from trial *and* error, and given common sense your errors will be few and your experience will soon grow. Just keep your ego out of it!

PROBLEMS

The problems for short tours must be minimal, barring accidents. If it starts to snow heavily, then good map work will prove beneficial. You can get very wet if snow gets under your clothing, so put on your windproofs, slow the speed, and seal your clothing at neck and wrist with scarl and gloves. If the visibility gets very bad, and you are in a dangerous position, move even more slowly, best skiers at front and rear.

If you get wet, providing you can stay warm, then stay wet. Keep your dry clothing until the evening. If you are wet but warm you will be fine — but if you get wet *and cold,* then put on dry clothing, for the risk of frost-nip or frostbite is too great.

8 · Longer ski tours

An extended ski tour can last from a few days to a few weeks. At that level it requires organization and pre-planning in an increasing degree, and it is fair to say that the more effort you put into the preparation, the more enjoyment you will get from the actual event.

EXPERIENCE
Before you embark on a long tour you should be competent in ski touring at a daily level. This itself, as we saw in the opening chapter, depends on a sound basic knowledge of outdoor skills plus, by now, a grasp of winter camping, ski techniques and navigation.

You should have had considerable day touring experience, plus a few overnight stops before you plan your large expedition.

COMPANIONS
The ideal number for a winter trip is four. Two is too few for security, while with three one always seems to get left out, although three will fit neatly into a winter tent. Having said that, I usually go with just one chosen companion, a long-time friend, and we gain in harmony what we lack in numbers. It is advisable to be SURE that the group is harmonious and at about the same level of skill. This does not mean that everyone is *equally* experienced in *everything*. If it did, no one would ever get a start, but it does mean that the level of skills is such that everyone can pull his or her weight, and add to the effectiveness of the group. All should ski at about the same level and speed, if only by agreement, or the group will split up, but if, say, there is only one good map reader, but he or she if balanced by one good cook, the whole group benefits and the others can share the chores. Above all, you must get on together. Quarrels on the trail are a nuisance, but in my experience, mercifully rare.

INFORMATION
Unless you are lucky enough to live in the middle of a ski-touring area, large enough to absorb all your energy and small enough to offer totally similar conditions and terrain, you will often have to ski in unknown areas. You can, of course, go on a tour with a company which specializes in winter touring. I would approve if this is your first tour in an unknown area. However, in that case you don't need my advice, for the tour operator will tell you what to bring, make all the arrangements, and even provide a guide. When you eventually go on your own though, you must make these arrangements for yourself. Personally, I enjoy these tasks and like the planning, and a trip to an unknown area gives me a great sense of adventure.

The first step is to assemble as much information as possible. Organize it under various headings, for example:-

1. Area, population, getting there.
2. Height, terrain details.
3. Snow cover, depth, avalanche record.
4. Weather, temperatures, wind direction.
5. Transport details, in, out and through.
6. Towns, villages and stores, food supplies.
7. Accommodation available.
8. Trails available.
9. Details of maps, contour interval, variation, etc.
10. Medical facilities and requirements.

Information on these subjects can be obtained from a number of sources and all should be tapped. Here are just a few you might approach.

1. Embassies.
2. Tourist Offices.
3. Alpine or ski clubs.
4. Outdoor magazines.
5. Library and Reference libraries.
6. Trail Guides.
7. Airlines.
8. Previous expeditions.
9. Friends.

Use your imagination and you will soon see a way to find out what you need to know. For detailed help on specific queries write to outdoor magazines, periodicals, etc., and ask them to publish your letters asking for information from people who have previously skied your chosen area, preferably recently. Get out a list and detail party members to collect all available information.

In my experience you cannot have to much information, and you need to check it carefully. It is extremely hard to get the *little* details, the apparently minor points which no one thinks worth mentioning but which can make or break your trip. They enable you to judge the amount of kit you need to take. As an example, do the huts have stores? Can you cook and do they have cutlery? Is there transport to the start? Does it run in winter? Is the snow deep enough for snowholes? Are there places to stock up with food en route? Can you buy petrol or replace used gas cylinders? One of the advantages, but also one of the snags, is that many excellent ski touring areas are also summer hiking or backpacking areas. The advantage is that a trail and hut network exists, but the snag is that much of the information given relates to the summer and if you rely on it for the winter, you may get a nasty shock. You must check and double check, for people will tell you as firm facts the most outrageous nonsense. You may have to say, *"Yes, yes, but what about the winter"* before the light dawns and your informant admits *"Well No, of course not, it doesn't open/work in winter".* Of course!

If, in the end, to avoid the risk of error, you take everything you need for every situation, you end up carrying a great deal of unnecessary gear. One way to avoid falling down this particular crevasse is to make a reconnaissance, preferably in the early winter, or the previous year, but this tends to waste precious vacation time, although you can always day tour one year, and once you know the area, return for a long trip.

RECONNAISSANCE

Failing this, one other way is to visit the region in summer. The locals will tell you about the region in winter, and their information is *probably* — not *definitely*, accurate. You can inspect the facilities and find out from the people who run them what will and what will not be open in winter. You can also make arrangements about food, transport and any necessary back-up, including guides. I recently arranged a winter tour, across fairly wild country, and found many farms, unmarked as such on the maps, while on the reconnaissance. The farmers were more than willing to offer us accommodation in the forthcoming winter, thus providing the missing links for our proposed tour. If you can make a reconnaissance, you would be well advised to do so, but follow up your verbal arrangements with a letter, and check, check and check again, right up to the last minute.

TRANSPORT

Getting to the start of your tour can be a problem. If you drive or hire a car to get into the hills, remember to have it equipped with snow-tyres, or at least snow chains, and have a shovel and a few sacks with you in case you get stuck. A warning red triangle is necessary in many countries, but snow chains can usually be hired locally. Here again, check.

If you propose leaving your car for a week or more, be sure it will start again when you return to it. Leave it in a garage rather than the open, or get some friendly farmer to put it in his barn. The cost, if spread among four people will be worth it. Even if the car is already 'winterised' with anti-freeze, the solution needed in the hills may well need to exceed the percentage of glycol you normally use if you live in a lowland area.

Starting can be a real problem after a stay in deep cold, and spray additives in the tank can be useful. When setting off, leave the car in gear, but if possible with the brakes off, for they can freeze in the 'on' position, and be difficult to relese.

The windscreen and locks may freeze up, so spray them with antifreeze before you go and tape over the keyholes. A spare set of keys is also useful. Finally, have the car properly serviced before you go off and drive carefully on those icy mountain roads, especially when tired and in a hurry to get home.

If you are heading to your area by air or sea, remember that winter weather can close airports and delay ferries, so allow time for this. A tight schedule in winter is usually inadvisable.

FOOD

Food can be a problem when touring. Other items, clothes, skis and equipment can be re-used, but once you have eaten your food you have to replace it. Food is a limiting factor but you have to eat. So, what can we do?

One way round it is simply to carry extra food. People on a long tour in the Arctic regions may have no choice but to carry heavy packs, but other alternatives are available, so consider the following:

1. You can cache food on the trail at points where you cut roads. The food must be sealed in airtight tins, and buried in some clearly marked spot. If you are running a lateral trail you can make your caches dropping off food as you run up the start point. If your route crosses roads, establish caches from a car. If this seems too primitive or risky, you can leave supplies with hut wardens or on farms, if you want lightweight foods, but in such cases you can often buy fresh food

anyway. If you leave a cache, mark the place with sticks and a scrap of cloth. Stones may soon be covered with fresh snow.

2. You can use a sled if you must carry lots of food and wish to reduce the pack load. Many long expeditions pack all their heavy stores on sleds, and food supplies for a long trip can be easily transported like this. This is, to my mind, an extreme case, and I imagine that the bulk of the readers will never need to haul sleds like turn-of-the-century Arctic explorers. But it's an idea to consider if your plan needs lots of supplies.

For the bulk of ski tours it remains sufficient to fix a replenishment point every three or four days, and stop in these for fresh supplies. These stops add great variety to the tour, and you will enjoy the sight of people and maybe the chance for a shower and a drink.

EQUIPMENT
Weight is the real problem. You can cut the weight considerably by sharing items and given good pre-trip planning this can be done without extra risk.

On a recent tour my kit was as follows:-

Worn;
1 pair ski boots.
1 pair Berghaus Goretex gaiters.
2 pairs loop stitch socks.
1 set 'Lifa' thermal underwear.
1 pair cord trousers.
1 cotton roll-necked sweater.
1 wool pullover (tied round waist)
1 fibre-pile jacket.
1 balaclava helmet.
1 pair ski gloves.
1 pair ski goggles.
1 camera.
1 compass.

I carried, in a 45 litre Millet rucksack, the following:-
1 Thermarest mattress.
1 down sleeping bag.
1 bivvy bag*.
2 sets (2 pairs per set) socks.
1 spare pair gloves*.
1 set Lifa underwear (for sleeping).
1 pair trousers (wool).
1 shirt (wool).
1 set Goretex windproofs.
2 pairs underpants.
6 rolls of film.
1 plastic plate.
1 × 1 litre water bottle.
1 torch plus spare bulb and battery.
1 candle.
2 boxes matches kept in 35mm film can.
1 ice axe*.
1 set heel crampons*.

The other two carried similar amounts of personal kit.

GROUP ITEMS

1 cookset.
1 Svea petrol stove.
2 litres white gas. One carried the stove, the other two a litre of fuel each.
2 days freeze-dried food.
1 tent, split into three loads*.
  (a) Tent
  (b) Fly
  (c) Poles & pegs.
1 set maps and trail guides.
1 snow shovel*.
1 first aid kit*.
1 set ski repair kit, including spare plastic tip, epoxy resin, binding, wishbone and screws*.

The starred items were not used or necessary for this trip, but some items, such as repair and first aid kit, must and will always be carried.

When all this was gathered on the floor, it made a fair pile, but divided into three loads it went easily into the rucksacks, and my personal load weighed 16lb. (7.3 kilos).

I have gone on tours carrying 30lb. and believe me, 16lb. is better. By and large, people tend to carry too much gear. Try to reduce it and take only what you *need*. You can go on adding to the above list, but ensure that you are covered for most eventualities. Given better knowledge of the terrain we could have dispensed with some items, but then again, the weather could have turned nasty. We felt content and no one complained.

This is one man's opinion, but I have met parties touring for a week in the Alps, carrying 14lb. apiece, and people carrying 70lb. plus. The choice is still yours, but my advice is to strain every effort to keep the weight down to 20lb. or less.

I do not offer this as the optimum kit list for every trip. For example we took no avalanche cord or sonde, no binoculars, no snowshoes. Had we considered these items remotely necessary we would have taken all or some of them on a group basis. The reconnaissance said they would, on this trip anyway, be superfluous. On the other hand, we took ice axe, tent and crampons, as safety items and never used them for that purpose, but the ice axe came in handy to chop ice for water. You must draw up your kit list to cope with the terrain, the length of the trip and your activities on the trail. This has to be *your* decision. No cut and dried list can cope with the trip you may be planning. *You must think for yourself.*

WINTER NAVIGATION

If you are an experienced backpacker, or cross country skier, you can often tell just by looking at the map if a trail will 'go'. Even so, a reconnaissance will help, for if you are running on 'skare' or frozen crust, you might want to alter your route to stay off steep icy slopes.

Accurate navigation in winter is essential. A mountain refuge is a small place in the wilderness and easily missed. It is a good idea, and will save hours of precious daylight, to work out your route to the next night stop with plenty of the relevant bearings and landmarks noted on the route card. This saves constant stops and much fiddling with the compass and map in a heavy wind. Don't do it for days ahead, as any plan must be flexible, and all sorts of conditions, weather, wind, snow state, weariness, can affect long term plans. Do it daily.

If you are off a waymarked trail, head for a clear unmistakable landmark, one that you cannot miss, near the refuge. 'Aim-off' to one side of your destination so that you know, on arriving at the landmark or in the area, where to look for your night stop, or which way to turn.
Visibility can change very quickly so the Golden Rule of map work, *"Always know where you are"* is doubley important in winter.

SAFETY RULES
Ski touring areas often litter their huts and refuges with safety leaflets and if the following rules were adhered to ski touring could expand without further controls. So pay attention to the following:-

1. Watch the weather. Have an escape route planned and if the weather thickens or gets foul take to it without delay.
2. Advise someone of your destination, chosen route and arrival time.
3. Don't forget to check in on arrival.
4. Never exceed your abilities, and be fit at the start.
5. Always carry a map and compass and know how to use them.
6. Be properly clad and carry some survival equipment at all times, including food, whistle, bivvy bag and torch.
7. Never go out alone.
8. If the weather is unfavourable, don't go out at all.

These are very simple, but if adhered to will save you a lot of worry at some time in your life.

A DAY ON THE TRAIL
Start early. Get up before daylight if possible and get away at first light. Time lost in the morning can never be made up. The snow will be frozen and you will make good time before the sun gets up and starts to melt it. Check the area or hut carefully before you leave for any forgotten items, and leave the place better than you found it. On the trail, take turns to break trail, lead, navigate and bring up the rear, but *stay together.* If someone continually ranges ahead, group decisions on routes, stops or problems become impossible.
Trail stops should be few, as you will tend to chill down, but eat *'nibbles'* regularly, drink a lot, and, if you stop for a brew, find a lee against the wind, or dig out a shelter with the shovel. If the wind is very cold, use barrier creams and remember *'frost nip'.*

END OF THE DAY
At the end of the day, if not before, you can be tired. Aim to have at least one hour's daylight from the time you stop to get organized. Fetch or melt snow or ice for water, and have a brew. If necessary get enough water ready for later brews and fill water bottles.
Once in your shelter, whether it be hut, tent or snow hole, lay out sleeping mats and bags, and get out of the skiing clothes and into your dry warm sleeping gear. Put your outdoor clothes, down boots or snow shoes and a torch where you can find them in the dark.
Now, eat a good sustaining meal before you settle down for the night. Before you go to sleep check the shelter, put your water supplies where they won't freeze again, and then good-night! It's another long day tomorrow.

9 · Winter living

If you go ski touring for more than a day, then you don't just ski out there on the snowfields — you must live out there. All the normal business of eating, sleeping, washing, going to the lavatory, and clearing up must be considered and performed, or the tour will either collapse, or become increasingly unpleasant for all concerned. Besides, unless you are competent at living out-of-doors in winter then extended ski touring is not possible, and even then, life must be reduced to the basics of shelter, sleep and food.

ACCOMMODATION

Outdoor people are often creatures of habit, and when they take up ski touring after summer walking or backpacking, they often adapt their summer habits to the winter role. This is fine, up to a point, but ski touring is different and you should consider adapting your normal habits to whatever is popular locally. The locals usually know best, and in nothing is this more true than in accommodation.

Apart from hotels, which all outdoors people rightly shun, (don't we?) ski touring accommodation can be divided into three main types. The first are the hostels, by which we can mean buildings with stone or wooden walls which can be called hostels, huts refuges, gites or bothies, depending on which nation's snowfield you are touring. The next option is a tent, and a tent is often carried as a group item anyway, for safety's sake; Finally, we have snow-holes or snow caves. These are often taught or just experienced as a survival medium, but if the snow is suitable, firm and deep enough, then a snowhole is the ideal base for touring an area. Digging a fresh snowhole every night when on a lateral point-to-point tour can be a considerable chore, but when touring out into the hills from a fixed point, they are quite useful. You can even build an igloo!

HOSTELS, HUTS

In many countries, particularly those with regular snowfalls, and long tradition of ski-touring, like Scandinavia, the long ski-touring trails or touring areas are well supplied with hostels. Some of these huts have wardens, some do not. Some have food supplies, some just offer shelter. Some are simple and some elaborate. It is important to find out just what degree of accommodation is available as this will affect the amount of food and equipment you need to carry. On the Grande Traversée of the Jura, for example, the huts or gites are well equipped with stoves and kitchens, but have no food. In Norway the wardens of the Den Norske Turistföring (DNT) pack opening supplies of food up to the huts in summer, and replenish them as the winter goes on. You just use what you want and pay for it, putting the money into a box. Nobody cheats.

In the Vercors region of France, the huts are primitive, with wide shelves

GROUNDSHEET COVERED WITH SNOW BLOCKS. SUPPORTED BY SKIS AND POLES OR BRANCHES.

IF USING SKIS LEAVE BINDINGS FACING DOWN.

FLAP DOOR

A SNOW TRENCH

instead of bunks. On the trails marked by the Adirondac Mountain Club in the Eastern USA the huts have bunks and a stove, but little else. The one point about huts is that, except for safety, you need not carry a tent, but huts do vary. You must find out who looks after the huts and get up-to-date information on what they contain.

CLUBS

If you want to go on a hut tour it is always polite, sometimes necessary and often less expensive, to join the local mountain or ski touring club, or an affiliated nature body in your own country. The Touring Club de France, The Austrian Alpine Club, the Youth Hostels Association, the Adirondac Mountain Club, the Club Alpin Français are just a few organizations, in different parts of the world, which run or maintain a hut network for summer hikers and winter tourers and these and many other national organizations often have affiliations with overseas clubs. Membership entitles you to lower fees for hut use, and you can reserve accommodation in manned hostels. I have never heard of any non-member being turned away into the blizzard, but you will certainly have to pay more, and will not be able to book ahead.

Find out all you can about available hostels (See Information Page 72), and even so, take tent or shovel. I have skied all day to reach one hut in the Vercors and found when I got there that it had burnt down!

TENTS

Tents are often taken out as a safety measure, and for such an occasion a three-season (Spring, Summer, Autumn) tent will do, provided it has a flysheet and you know how to winterise it properly. A good proofing agent or 'sealant' along the seams can make a lot of difference. Add a few extra guys as well, to cope with winter winds.

If, however, you *intend* to camp, or are touring an area with no huts and shallow snow cover, then you need a mountain tent. You may think that this special tent is a pure frill but if you become committed to touring, sooner or later you will be very glad you invested in a proper tent.

79

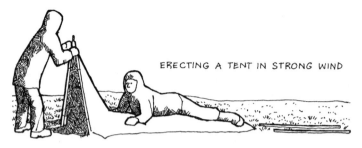

ERECTING A TENT IN STRONG WIND

A good tent, suitable for snow camping in severe conditions, would have a flysheet, with good porch to provide a cooking area and a wide flap or 'snow valance', around the walls. Single skin tents are not sufficient, but the available features vary.

An 'A' frame tent, with the poles leading through grommets in the wall and slotted through the base wall, is the most useful, for a pole if not fed through a grommet will sink steadily into the snow. A 'tunnel' entrance into the tent will keep out driving snow and cut draughts and a well-sloped roof, tightly pitched, will help shed snow, as will a ridgepole. A build up of wet, heavy snow on the tent can bring it down. New tent designs are coming out all the time, but buy a tent you can live in. You may have to get your group and all your gear, except skis, inside the tent, so too little room can be a nuisance. Some tents have a zip-out floor section to permit cooking inside the tent in a storm, but ventilation at all times is essential in a winter tent and cooking in the tent, if sometimes necessary is always dangerous. You will also need a range of snowholding pegs, and some people recommend an extra interior fly, or 'ice-liner', which absorbs frozen condensation.

WINTER PITCHES

Try and find a pitch a good hour before dark, in a safe, sheltered area, out of the wind and frost hollows, in the lee, but certainly not under trees or on an avalanche slope. Narrow valleys are wind tunnels, and side gulleys often avalanche paths. Stamp out the snow hard with the skis *on,* then take them off to tread the snow down even firmer with the boots. Pitch the tent, lying on it if the wind is blowing, and peg out the groundsheet windward side first. Use skis, ski poles and/or ice axes for the main guys, and snowholding pegs for the others. Freeze them in with a little water if neccessary. You can also attach a guy to a stuff sack, fill it with snow and bury it deep for extra security. Pile snow or snow blocks on the tent 'valance', and then build a snow wall around the entrance to give even more wind protection and to make a cooking area.

You must expect snow to pile up on the tent during the night, and you may have to dig yourself out in the morning, so take your shovel, and all other items you can, inside the tent, or they may either blow away or be buried. You can learn more about this subject from *'Snow Camping'* by Cameron McNeish, also published in this series.

STRIKING A TENT

If your tent has a fly leave the fly up until the last minute. The groundsheet may freeze to the ground after the campers leave it in the morning, so loosen the groundsheet while it is still warm. Pulling it loose will eventually ruin the outer proofing ! put my space blanket *under* the tent for this reason. Condensation or ice will also form as ice on the fly and, maybe, inside the main tent. It is almost impossible to keep blown snow out of the tent. Once in, it melts, and will refreeze as ice. You will try and brush off all you can, but it's something you learn to live with, but on a tent tour you will eventually get wet.

INSULATION, CONDENSATION, VENTILATION

To pass a warm night in a winter tent, put as much insulation as possible under you, on the floor of the tent. Cold strikes up from the ground. Newspapers are excellent and cheap insulation as are space blankets, bivvy bags, your windproofs or your spare clothing.

As the tent warms up, condensation will tend to develop on the inside. With a well-pitched fly, kept clear of the inner walls, much of the condensation will form there, but the inside of the tent can also get wet. Good ventilation is essential to minimise this nuisance and to prevent those other hazards that can arise from lack of oxygen or the build-up of carbon monoxide while cooking. I don't want to go on about this, but a 'good fug', while always pleasant, is not always wise. Remember to ventilate well.

SNOWHOLES

A shovel is an essential piece of ski touring equipment, carried as 'group' gear, for safety if for nothing else. You will find it useful for all sorts of purposes, and folding aluminium shovels weigh little and pack up well.

Snowholes are very cosy. If you have never tried one, this may surprise you, but it's true. I dislike being cramped up in a damp tent, and much prefer snowholing if the terrain permits. You can wile away the time carving cupboards in the walls, chiselling away at a shelf, or just tunnelling into the other snowhole next door for a chat.

TRENCHING

The simplest and quickest form of snowhole is the trench. You need even, deep snow (probe with your upturned ski pole) of firm but not icy consistency. You can, in emergency even kick out a trench or excavate one with the 'shovel' of the skis, but a proper snow shovel makes the task easier.

The trench should be about waist deep, two metres long and wide enough for two sleepers. You can tunnel out the sides at the bottom for extra storage space. Cover the top with skis, poles or branches, and use the tent fly, a cagoule, bivvy bag, or space blanket as the roof, covering this with snow for extra insulation.

This is not luxurious, but as an emergency shelter, trenches are quick to dig, very secure and windproof. Pile as much insulation as you can on the floor and remove your ski boots once you are in, to stop the floor getting too slushy. Put on overboots, and dry clothing when you are sure you won't have to go out again.

SNOWHOLES

For a long stay of several days or more, you can dig a proper snowhole in a steep bank or gully. Be sure you are not digging in an avalanche slope, or under a stonefall. Check the terrain carefully, and probe the snow with your reversed pole.

You can tunnel in and excavate a chamber at the end, but this will get

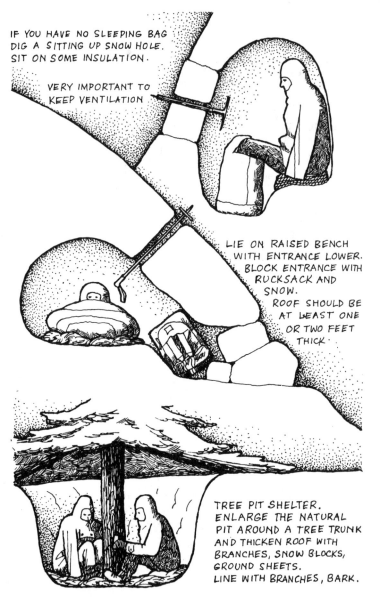

IF YOU HAVE NO SLEEPING BAG
DIG A SITTING UP SNOW HOLE.
SIT ON SOME INSULATION.

VERY IMPORTANT TO
KEEP VENTILATION

LIE ON RAISED BENCH
WITH ENTRANCE LOWER.
BLOCK ENTRANCE WITH
RUCKSACK AND
SNOW.
ROOF SHOULD BE
AT LEAST ONE
OR TWO FEET
THICK.

TREE PIT SHELTER.
ENLARGE THE NATURAL
PIT AROUND A TREE TRUNK
AND THICKEN ROOF WITH
BRANCHES, SNOW BLOCKS,
GROUND SHEETS.
LINE WITH BRANCHES, BARK.

you very wet, takes time and leaves the rest of the party standing about outside in the wind with nothing to do, since you can only dig one tunnel at a time. This Colditz technique can be very cold indeed.

It is better to dig out a cave, chopping your way into the snow until you have dug a semi-circular room. In this space you can get organized, and put on a brew. Then excavate a sleeping platform at the back about waist height, wide enough for 2 or 3 people, long enough for laying full length

82

plus rucksack, and high enough to sit up. Cold air will tend to settle on the floor and it will be warmer up on the platform. Use the excavated snow, or better still blocks cut while making the platform to fill in the outer entrance of the snowhole behind you, leaving a narrow door which, except for a ventilation hole, you can fill in at night or when you are out.

Digging snowholes takes a certain amount of time, but they can be very comfortable and the following points will help:-

1. Remove as much clothing as possible while digging, it is hot work and you get very wet.
2. Allow one shovel between two people, and snowhole in pairs. You can link up the holes later if you wish.
3. Don't forget ventilation. Sleep on a platform above the entrance draughts, and the 'cold' layer on the floor.
4. When you leave the snowhole to go skiing, close the entrance but mark it carefully. The entrance can be hard to find again.
5. If possible put fir branches on the floor for extra insulation.
6. Smooth off the roof and entrance passages. Any sharp edge will melt and drip. Curve the roof so that moisture runs down the walls.
7. Chop out recesses for stores, candle-niches, etc., but don't undermine the walls.
8. Take the shovel in and out with you in case you have to dig yourself out, or in again, after a snowfall.

Now that we have the accommodation settled we can get on with living.

EATING

Hot food is very comforting in the winter. If your hut has a stove you must wait your turn and clean up after you have used the cooking gear, so a swift snack may be helpful first. Remember to melt extra snow for water, using any spare heat, on pot lids, etc. to get the melt going. Chop wood to replace any firewood you use, and pay for your meals and any stores consumed. If you have spare food left at the end of your hut stay, leave some behind for those who follow you. Water can be a problem. Ice melts quicker than snow, and even faster if you add a little water. Smash the ice up small with your ice-axe or flail it with your crampons.

In tent or snowhole, you can clean the dishes with icy snow, and bury any scraps. Non-biodegradable items such as tins, foils and plastics, must be packed out. Burying trash in the snow simply preserves it until the Spring thaw.

Keep the food simple. Stews, thick soups, steamed puddings are quick to heat, preserving fuel and giving you plenty of nourishment. Some dehydrated foods can be difficult to use because of the water problem, but some freeze-dried foods are very good, light to carry and quick to prepare. Check on cooking methods and times before you buy. A snack before sleep will help to keep you warm, but you should not go to sleep until all water containers are filled, snow is melting in a plastic bag, and your water bottle is placed where it will not freeze again, which may mean inside your sleeping bag and inside a sock. Water is a necessity for any sort of meal, as you will soon discover.

SLEEPING

Don't sleep in your ski gear. It is certain to be damp from perspiration or blown snow. Once you are firmly inside for the night, change into your sleeping clothes, putting ski boots and parka nearby in case you have to go out again.

Shake the bag and lay it out early, so that the filling has time to 'loft'. Wearing a hat can help you stay warm, and socks help the feet. Plenty of insulation under you will be more effective than piling spare clothing on top of the bag.

LAVATORIES

When you gotta go — you gotta go! Methods vary depending on facilities and the weather, but it is not a subject you can ignore. A wide-necked P-Bottle of adequate capacity, marked 'NON-POTABLE' is one idea, and a blessing on a cold night after too many brews! In daytime, pee-ing on the snow does no harm but don't melt yellow snow! For more complicated matters you may have to rely on the shovel, a windbreak and desperation.

If you are the type who likes to retire to the lavatory with a good book, then hard luck, or change your habits. Swiftness is all. In particularly bad weather you just don't! I recall skiing ten miles off the hill in terrible weather to find a friendly cafe, and it was the sort of group decision which makes friends for life. Self-induced constipation is not something to encourage, so take every opportunity for comfort whatever the temperature, and remember that bothy or hut lavatories, even the earth closet type, must be kept clean.

WASHING AND CLEANING

Try and keep clean. Beards, while popular, are something of a menace. They collect snow, and the skin beneath can freeze without detection. Anyway, if you like to feel clean you have to shave. I use a battery operated razor, but I try and wash my hands, face and neck once a day at least with a warm flannel, even in tent or snowhole. Put on a barrier cream after shaving or washing or your skin will chap. Hut facilities vary, but if you can have a decent wash or shower, then do so.

On an extended tour it is not a bad idea, as on a summer backpacking trip, to descend to the valley at least once a week, for a shower and a chance to wash out and dry underwear. Washing clothes on a tour, even drying out wet socks, is rarely practical, outside a hut. You may be able to sling a line up over the stove or in the kitchen, but most huts get pretty cold at night. Some French *gites d'etape* have central heating, showers and drying rooms, but this would be the exception. On the whole the *vie* is *primitif*.

ATTITUDE

It is perfectly possible, by choosing your area, to tour from hotel to hotel. If that is what pleases you, then that is your privilege, and it is still ski touring. If you strike out on your own then it is necessary to reduce your requirements to the minimum, and the right attitude to winter living is important. You should accept discomfort only in so far as it is unavoidable. When you have done all you can to ensure your safety, shelter, warmth, food and a good night's sleep, you have all the elements necessary to stay out, and need nothing more. If you want luxury, this is not the place for it, but the satisfaction and the sheer pleasure, not only in getting back to the creature comforts, but also in realizing you can do without them, is not to be lightly dismissed. Winter living is a pleasant sort of pain in the neck!

10 · Hazards

If you are reasonably experienced out-of-doors, you should be able to anticipate, recognize and so avoid, the usual hazards which await travellers in remote areas. You will have followed, as a matter of course, all the usual procedures, and have the common sense necessary to cope with any unexpected problem which may arise. We assumed that in the first chapter, and of course there is no need to ski into remote regions at all. For the outdoors man or woman taking up ski touring, there are however two areas which present less common dangers and which repay extra consideration. The first problem is cold, and the second, a requirement following on from this element is a sound knowledge of winter hazards and how to avoid them.

SLIPS
Slips, due to wet rock, ice, wearing unsuitable footwear or any combination of the three, are a major cause of mountain accidents.

It is commonplace to remove the skis and walk when touring, if the path is too steep or icy and at this point a slip becomes at least a possibility.

The tourer has two allies against slips, crampons and ice axes. Put on your crampons before they are necessary and make sure they fit. They are not the ultimate answer, for they can 'ball-up' in wet snow, and need to be kept clean by rapping the boots together or banging the crampons with the ice axe.

WALKING IN CRAMPONS
Crampon technique takes practice. They should always be worn with gaiters or the spikes can snag on your flapping trousers. Gaiter laces should be tucked away for the same reason.

Outside ice climbing techniques which are not within my province, the more spikes you can get on the snow the firmer your grip will be. The tourer will climb the slope, traversing from side to side, and placing the sides of the feet so that all spikes grip. The ice axe is carried on the inside and the spike dug deep for extra security. Have the ice axe loop well coiled around the wrist. Front-pointing, on 12-point crampons is a useful ice-climbing technique, but any ski tourer who needs to use it is in a certain amount of trouble. What are you *doing* there?!

Coming down is also a matter for caution, and the ice axe should be planted deep ahead to give security as you move down.

STEP KICKING
On thin crust or wet snow you may not need crampons. You can kick steps in the snow, and a good deep kick, burying the foot to the ankle, gives good support. Be careful to kick ahead, horizontally, so that the foot is flat to the fall line and will not slip from the hole as you put weight on it.

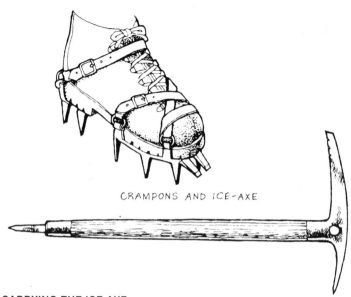

CRAMPONS AND ICE-AXE

CARRYING THE ICE AXE
The adze, pick and spike of the axe should be protected off the hill and on the rucksack, with rubber stoppers. Methods of carrying the axe vary, but the most accepted method is by the head, like a walking stick pick forward, spike down, until you get onto a steep slope and can carry the axe for use as a possible brake, in which case the axe should be carried across the body, head at shoulder height, pick down.

STEP CUTTING
If the surface is too hard for step kicking, then you will have to cut steps with the ice axe. This is hard work, and is a skill worth practising. It helps if you are wearing crampons (as you should be) for even a well cut step is not entirely secure, and can give under your weight.

Swing the axe, straight armed from the shoulder, aiming to cut a shallow step with the adze, long enough for a boot.

The cut must be vertical to the fall line, and provided you can get the side of the boot secure you can step up and move on.

You can wield the axe with either arm, so choose whichever feels easier and most secure.

If the snow or ice is very hard you may need to cut a deep slot, enough for the whole boot. Practise this skill on your day tours, until you feel proficient not only at cutting steps, but also at ascending and descending slopes while using them. Practise should be carried out on a small slope with a clear safe run out at the bottom.

BRAKING WITH THE ICE AXE
An ice axe, as you will have noted has many uses. Extra tent peg, ice breaker, step cutter. Over and above all this it is carried for use as a brake in case of a slip. This is an important winter walking technique and it must be learned and practised regularly, on some short safe slope.

There are several techniques, and it is worth learning them all, but I will give just one here, which illustrates the main points.

The so-called *shoulder brake* calls for the axe to be carried across the body, head at shoulder level, the other hand low on the shaft. In the event of a slip the pick may either be driven into the crust as you fall, for an immediate brake, or if you are not ready to brake and already sliding, get the axe ready first, one hand at the head, one hand at the spike, and then engage the pick, apply pressure and body weight gradually, until the pick bites and you stop.

Frankly, it is not all that easy, and takes practice. Three points to watch for are as follows:-

1. Do not let the arms get over your head. You will not be able to get the pick in and may lose the axe.
2. If you are moving and try and slam the pick in it may bounce off the snow. Use your weight to press it home gradually.
3. If you are wearing crampons (as you should be) lift the feet high as you slide, or the points will catch and send you cartwheeling.

A slip is likely on steep icy slopes. Have the axe ready in such places, the spike trailing against the crust on the inside, and the axe head held pick down, ready for immediate use. If you slip, concentrate on keeping the hands low so that the body is over the axe, giving you the necessary weight.

Some say that the loop should not be around the wrist, but I believe the risk of a crack on the head is preferable to losing the axe. Even if you slide down safely, you still have to climb up again and will need the axe to do so.

Practise braking, you will feel much happier when you *know* you can stop.

FATIGUE & ACCLIMATIZATION

Winter travelling can be hard work. An extended tour has to be based on sound physical fitness, and if necessary, by special training for longer tours. Winter weather and continual effort can sap your strength, so the possibility exists that you will tire quicker in winter than you would over a similar distance in summer.

A speed of four miles an hour over open country on skis, is the *maximum* you should expect. With heavy packs and over broken country you can expect to manage much less. Either way, it is a fundamental mistake if you try to do too much. Stay cool, move easy, and avoid excessive perspiration.

Winter days are shorter, and it often takes longer to pack up and get going so you should anticipate covering *no more* than 20 miles per day on skis, in the best conditions, unless you are out to break records or have some desperate need to forge on. It's supposed to be fun. Height acclimatization must also be considered.

It may be necessary to go high to find adequate snow cover. At over 5,000 feet you can expect some slight problems with breathlessness, and lack of drive, and until you are used to the height these problems will increase with altitude.

Over 10,000 feet you will certainly need some time to acclimatize to the thinner air. I have skied at over 12,000 feet in the Andes and found it exhausting, while sleep for the first night or two proved impossible. I woke up panting after just a few minutes. This problem disappeared after a few days but remember not to plan great exertions in the first few days, especially over a distance and at height.

WINTER WEATHER
In winter, the weather is always a hazard. Even a sunny spell can cause problems, melting the crust and making your easy run a heavy slog, but be it changeable or just steadfastly cold, *NEVER NEGLECT TO OBTAIN AND ACT UPON WEATHER INFORMATION.*

Listen to the radio, obtain up to date forecasts, and obey avalanche warnings. Learn to read the weather signs, from cloud formations or changes in the wind (you should have this skill before you start ski touring).

Before planning a long tour, start collecting weather information several days before so that some pattern can be established, and up-date these forecasts at every opportunity, by asking other tourers you encounter, or enquiring at mountain huts. A small transistor radio might be useful for this purpose, but reception in the hills is often difficult, and the cold can affect the batteries. Just keep your weather eye open, at all times.

WIND CHILL
Every outdoor person knows that the chilling effect of a cold day is multiplied by the wind. This fact is scientific. *"The wind chill factor"* operates in low temperatures from about 40°F (8°C) down to about − 40°F. Below this the extra chilling due to wind speed is negligible, but below this temperature you will have problems enough anyway.

Personally I take great trouble to counteract wind chill, staying off exposed ridges whenever possible, wearing a hat and gloves, and putting on windproofs when the wind gets up. The wind, even at 0°C can drop the real temperature dramatically. One winter, crossing the Appalachian Gap in the USA. we found that an air temperature of 32°F in shelter dropped to about 1°F out in the wind. That is 30°F below freezing! And that's cold! Our faces were whipped red and chapped within a very few minutes, before we retreated. Use natural cover to cut the direct effect of wind, stay below crests and circle to keep in the lee of trees. Wear a face mask, *and* a layer of barrier cream in such conditions, and wrap up well. Study this chart.

WIND CHILL CHART

Wind Speed	Local Temperature (F)			
0	32	23	14	5
5	29	20	10	1
10	18	7	− 4	− 15
15	13	− 1	− 13	− 25
20	7	− 6	− 19	− 32
30	1	− 13	− 27	− 41

Note then, and don't forget, that the *effective* temperature can, thanks to the wind, be much lower than the true air temperature and this can lead to such irritations as chapped skin, cracked lips, frost nip and even more serious, frostbite, but correct clothing can greatly reduce, or nullify the wind chill factor.

WHITE-OUTS AND BLIZZARDS

A *'white-out'* occurs in the hills when low clouds merge with the snowy landscape to create a situation where visibility is nil and landmarks, even close to, are undefined.

To ski in such a situation is difficult and even dangerous, and the party must keep well closed up together and proceed slowly, if at all. If the wind is beind you, you can snake your *oertal* cord out in front to give some idea of dips or crevasses. Use the compass to maintain direction in such conditions.

Blizzards can be even more of a problem. If the wind is driving the snow hard, it may be as well to stop and settle down in tent or snowhole until it stops. This can, of course, take days in the most extreme cases, but usually a blizzard will blow itself out in a day or two at the most.

Heavy snow can collapse the walls of your tent, and it may be necessary to emerge from time to time and scrape it off. You can easily become snowed in in your hut or snowhole, which is *another* reason to take a shovel into your shelter with you: in order to dig yourself out.

Movement in low visibility has to be by reckoning time and distance. Use your watch to give you a 'time on trail', and your compass to maintain direction. If you feel that you cannot reach your destination, then you must return to your previous point on a back-bearing, or stop where you are, and wait out the night or the snow storm. Pressing on when conditions are poor usually leads to more trouble.

DEHYDRATION

One little realized effect of hard effort in low temperatures, is physical dehydration, and thirst. Cold air is dry, containing less moisture than even moderatley dry, warm air. You will therefore perspire freely, and so dehydrate quite rapidly. It is important to take plenty of fluids, and it is better to drink tea or even plain water rather than coffee which is a diuretic. Ski tourers will soon notice that they pass very little water, a significant indication of the fluid they are losing through dehydration. Drink plenty and you will feel stronger.

FROSTNIP AND FROSTBITE

Frostnip is the first stage of frostbite and both can be prevented. Frostnip usually shows at the extremeties, in the toes, fingers, ear lobes and cheeks. These will go numb, lose all sense of feeling, and may appear white or patchy, but such areas can usually be re-warmed without much ill effect. Frostbite, which will follow if the 'frostnip' situation is allowed to continue and develop is much more serious, involving as it does an actual freezing of the flesh.

The prime causes of frostbite are exposure to wind chill, tight clothing or bootlaces restricting circulation, wetting in low temperatures by falling or treading in a stream, or by contact with freezing objects, metals or ice. Hypothermia can also cause frostbite, as the blood leaves the limbs in an attempt to keep the body-core warm.

So, *RULE No.1: Always anticipate the possibility of frostbite in low temperature — wind chill conditions.*

The signs of frostbite are:-

1. Numbing of the affected part(s).
2. Loss of sensation.
3. Blanching or white patches on the skin or cheeks.

Keep an eye on each other for these tell-tale signs.

If these signs are spotted early, the part can and must be covered or chafed back into warmth without delay. If your feet get wet in freezing weather stop at once, dry them and change the socks. Put up the tent or dig a shelter while you do this if necessary. Fingers can be warmed in the groin or armpit while if the feet or toes are numb they can be placed on the belly of a co-operative friend — this, as they say, is when you find out who your *real* friends are.

If true frostbite develops you have a very serious problem. The freezing will probably extend deep into the flesh and some tissue loss is at least possible.

If the worst happens, do not try and re-warm frostbitten limbs, on the trail unless you can stop completely and send out for help. It is better to walk to medical assistance on frozen feet. Improper or incomplete warming of a frostbitten part will result in great pain and further tissue damage, and in any event proper medical treatment will be required. Do *NOT* rub a frostbitten limb or flesh with frozen snow.

The basic treatment, which is best carried out under medical supervision, is to place the affected part in an 'elbow-warm' bath of water at between 100-110°F, certainly no higher. Even after rewarming, a frostbitten casualty will have problems, their gravity depending on the extent of the damage.

Prevention is clearly much better than painful cure, so wear the proper clothing and keep the extremeties warm. Beware of wind-chill and loosen tight laces on boots to help blood flow easily. The tight straps of heavy packs can restrict circulation to arms and the fingers. Beards are a frostbite danger, as the chill on the face beneath cannot be seen.

HYPOTHERMIA

Hypothermia is a more subtle enemy. I have experienced it only once, the main sign on that occasion being an inability to keep on my feet. I had stayed up very late, drunk a whole cup of coffee for breakfast and forgotten to wear my hat and windproofs, a fairly classic combination of errors.

The condition referred to as 'exposure' is caused by inadequate protection against cold, wet and wind conditions. On their own, neither of these three need bother the skier. In combination they can be lethal, so you must take steps to counter their effects. Hypothermia, which can be the end result of exposure, is severe loss of body core heat, and can cause death.

Prevention is, as always, the best answer. Correct clothing, regular food, and adequate rest, will help you avoid exposure. The symptoms of exposure develop slowly at first but then with increasing severity and rapidity. Uncharacteristic behaviour, stumbling, speaking in a slurred voice, becoming withdrawn or sullen, stupidity, sudden bursts of chatter and laughter, listlessness, may be the first signs of exposure, so don't shrug them off. Once the victim collapses you have a severe problem.

TREATMENT

Once the symptoms are suspected or detected, STOP and get out of the wind. If the victim is in the early stages and still conscious, get him or her warm. Make a shelter or a windbreak. Get the casualty into windproofs, and if they are available get him into dry clothes. Cover up the head and hands, because at least thirty per cent of the body's heat loss is from the head, and if he is still conscious give him a hot drink from your vacuum flask. If possible, get him into a sleeping bag. If you are on a day tour you probably won't have one, but a large plastic bivvy bag is an excellent substitute, particularly if it's large enough for someone else to get in beside the victim for extra warmth. The hypothermia victim *must* be rewarmed as quickly as possible.

If the victim is unconscious, then the situation is very serious and medical aid should be obtained as quickly as possible. Do not force any drinks into an unconscious person. Do not leave the victim alone or unattended, and remember that warmth is the best treatment. The basic rule in cases of exposure is to re-warm the victim as fast as is reasonably possible, while excluding the elements which caused the condition to arise. Shelter, rest and warmth are the answers to the condition, while food, proper clothing and not attempting too much in bad weather are the best precautions.

WETTING
In summer, if you get wet you stay wet — until you get dry. In winter wet clothes are extremely uncomfortable, and in wind chill conditions a wetting can be deadly. So, stay dry, for dry means warmth.

If, for example, you put your foot through the snow down into a hidden stream, stop and change your socks and the inner sole of your boot. If you go in up to your waist, and don't relish stripping off in the open snowfields, then have the tent pitched and change inside. If you have no spare clothes — (you fool!) — put on your windproofs over the top and keep moving. Then you will be wet-warm as opposed to wet-frozen. Down clothing loses all insulation once it gets wet, so try not to let this happen. Wet, driving, snow can soak you, so don't wait to put on your windproofs.

ANOXIA
Shelters contain their own range of hazards, due to the fact that it is nice to close up all the entrances against the chill and get a nice warm fug going inside. People die like that, for the air runs out or becomes saturated with fuel fumes. The basic error of poor ventilation is compounded by burning oil lights, and using stoves or lamps, which give off fumes. NEVER cook or use flame lights without adequate ventilation and always have *some* air flowing into the shelter.

The carbon-monoxide gas produced as a by-product by most stoves is colourless and odourless. You won't detect it until you keel over. Anoxia, which simply means 'lack of oxygen', can occur in quite large huts when too many people crowd in and close up all the vents. Flickering candle flames are a good indication or decreasing oxygen supply in the air. I can't say that this is a major hazard, but it's one to remember. You can get a bad headache at the very least.

Fire remains a danger in winter, as much as in summer, and if your hut or tent burns down destroying your stores, then you are in serious trouble. Be careful when filling, lighting or using stoves of lamps. Experienced people know this, but accidents still occur.

CREVASSES
On open slopes, deep frozen snow or glaciers, crevasses are always possible. Snow bridges frequently span these gulfs, but are not to be trusted unless they are thick and the gap narrow. Rope up if you have a

rope with you, and spread out to disperse the weight. Without a rope go higher, cross at a narrow gap, or, better still retreat.

AVALANCHES
Avalanche accidents are becoming more common. This is due as much as anything to the fact that more people are travelling deeper into the winter hills and putting themselves at risk. There always were avalanches, but now there are people in the way.

Most of the people killed or maimed by avalanches are skiers. Downhill skiers have some protection as they operate on prepared runs, under the watchful eye of local people and safety teams. Ski Patrols not only mark out safe runs, but remove impending dangers, often dislodging possible avalanches with dynamite. The best way to remove an impending avalanche is to create one first, and the 'boom' of explosions doing just that is a common sound in the mountains in winter.

CARELESSNESS AND STUPIDITY
Most of the people killed every year are killed by carelessness. They fail to use their common sense, ignoring warning signs, skiing round barriers, and running across avalanche slopes. Even warnings from Ski Patrols are ignored or shrugged off. Sometimes the first skiers get away with it and their tracks, curving across that inviting slope, lure others out onto it and to their deaths. So, more rules — NEVER:-

1. Ignore avalanche warnings.
2. Ski past barriers, or on closed routes.
3. Ignore the advice of instructors, guides or avalanche teams.

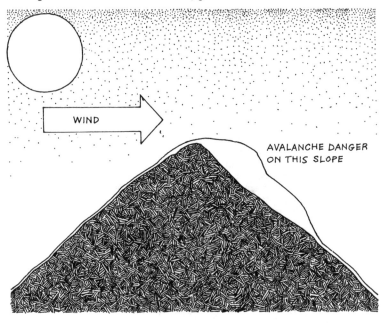

WIND

AVALANCHE DANGER ON THIS SLOPE

TYPES OF AVALANCHE

Avalanches can occur almost anywhere. Tree-covered slopes, with a gradient of less than 15° can avalanche. People have been killed by avalanches less than 20 metres wide, flowing only a hundred yards. The snow collapsed under them, swallowed them up, settled over them and the pressure forced it to freeze, burying them alive.

AVALANCHE PATHS

This said, some areas are more risky than others. Steep gulleys are natural avalanche paths. North or east facing slopes can be dangerous, if the temperature rises sharply. Beware of slopes between 2000 and 3000 metres high. Convex slopes are marginally more risky than concave ones, but even shallow gulleys are high risk areas. Overhanging ice or rock creates a risk, because a stone or icicle, even dripping water can trigger the slope below. A fall of new snow, *particularly* if it is heavy, can, as it settles, slip from the old base snow, and avalanche. Provided the rate of slide is slow and the snow dry and light, loose snow avalanches are not too dangerous, but if the slope is long and the speed builds up it can develop into the next, and a very lethal, variety, the airborne powder avalanche.

AIRBORNE-POWDER AVALANCHE

In these, the snow gains momentum, flies into the air at increasing speed, and creates a terrific wind blast and suction. They travel at great speed, up to 200 mph and can be amazingly destructive, shattering buildings, stripping trees from a slope, hurling buses and cars from roads. They are not unlike localized hurricanes. One such avalanche struck a bus-load of skiers in Switzerland and killed 24 out of the 35 people on board.

WET SNOW AVALANCHES

These are most common in the Spring when the temperature rises and the snow melts. They tend to be slow, but are heavy, and skiers caught in them will be crushed to death. Luckily they are slow, often follow regular routes, and occur at a predictable time of the year and likely slopes are often closed to skiers.

SLAB AVALANCHES

These happen when a complete slab of snow breaks away in a unit, and plunges into the valley. They often occur on or over open slopes, and can come from snow packed into slabs by wind action.

Slab snow is always dangerous because the wind action has formed it into a mass, without having blended it to the base beneath. It is therefore hanging up there by its own weight, and even the slightest pressure or movement can loosen it. Skiers are at particular risk from this sort of avalanche, for the snow looks so even and attractive that they are tempted on to it. Wind-driven slab snow should be avoided.

AVALANCHE PRECAUTIONS

The best precaution is to use common sense, listen to advice, and obey any signs or warnings, even your own 'feelings'.

Cross country skiers, whose favoured terrain is often country where avalanches occur, should always travel in parties, but only cross slopes singly, having deployed an oertal cord behind them. An oertal cord is a length of red line marked with direction arrows which you trail behind you.

If you go under there is a good chance that this line will still be visible on the surface and you can be located before you suffocate.

Before you cross a worrying slope, try and test it first, by shouting, or throwing stones or snowballs out on to the snow. If nothing happens, loosen the pack straps, remove the hands from the pole loops, and cross singly. The one on the slope should be watched by the rest, even by those who have already crossed safely. If the slope carries someone away, watch where he disappears. If you feel the slope going you *may* have a few seconds to get rid of skis and poles. The snow wrenching them round can fracture your arms and legs. Try 'swimming' on your back to stay near the surface or 'rolling' to stay at the edge of the slide. This actually works. Keep the mouth shut, and as the slide slows, try and clear a space around the mouth and chest to give you breathing room. Snow is usually porous and you will have sufficient air.

Those on the surface should first search the slope below where the victim was last seen, before sending for an avalanche team. Speed is essential in avalanche rescue, and efforts must start at once.

There is a lot more to learn about avalanches and this outline is only designed to alert you to the danger. Perhaps this little knowledge, which is not always a dangerous thing, will come in useful one day. To learn more I recommend that you read Colin Fraser's excellent *'Avalanches and Snow Safety'* (John Murray 1978) or, if you prefer a fictional but factually correct thriller, read Desmond Bagley's *'The Snow Tiger'* (Fontana 1976).

CORNICES

A cornice is a ridge of wind-packed snow projecting out over a cliff or crest. Cornices are inherently unstable and the cause of many winter accidents. They often obscure a view and so tempt you to climb up on to it at which moment it can break away. Moreover, cornices break at an angle away from the crest, so you may be carried over when well away from the true edge of the cliff or escarpment.

Cornices collapse can trigger an avalanche. I know of two ski tourers who were engulfed when climbers above them broke a cornice and triggered the slope. So if you see climbers above you, don't stop and stare, move on and get out from under.

FIRST AID IN THE COLD

The elements of First Aid, which all outdoor people capable of using this book should already know, remain basically the same in winter, but cold compounds the effects of injury.

Shock always results in a loss of body warmth. The blood will flow to the affected part, diluting the supply to the extremeties, and leading to further chilling. Tourniquets should not be used in any case, but are particularly dangerous in winter as they can result in an increased risk of frostbite to the blood starved limb. For the same reason, tight bandaging must be discouraged.

When carrying a casualty out, keep the victim well covered. He or she can get very cold on a stretcher and so if the casualty has to be carried out he or she should be placed in a sleeping bag. The cold has no charity and will seize any chance to add to your problems. Take cold into account, when treating any injury.

CONCLUSIONS

I don't want to finish this book with a list of woes and dangers. Ski touring is great fun and you will enjoy it. That is the be-all-and-end-all of this winter pastime and today is not too soon to start.

You have here all the basics, and as you learn them well and gain experience you will find that ski touring is full of opportunities and excitement, a sport which can take you to remote and beautiful places, in many parts of the world.

Finally, since this is the hazards chapter, let us give a few rules.

The Norwegians, who after all originated ski touring, have a sensible set of rules.

DO YOU KNOW THESE NINE MOUNTAIN RULES?

1. Don't go for long trips unless you are fit.
2. Always leave word where you're going.
3. Look at the weather and listen to the forecasts.
4. Don't be a know-all — pay attention to the voice of experience.
5. Storms can occur on short trips too. Bring rucksack and equipment essential in the mountains. On longer trips, don't forget a shovel.
6. Never forget your map and compass.
7. Never go alone.
8. Don't be afraid to turn back before it is too late.
9. Seek shelter in time or dig in to conserve your energy.

And, oh yes, Rule No.10, enjoy yourself.

The snow is always with us, a master, a danger, and a friend. Try it and you'll like it, I promise.

Bibliography

The following publications will provide detailed information on all aspects of the outdoors in winter, and should be consulted.

Avalanches and Snow Safety, Colin Fraser (John Murray U.K. 1978)
Avalanche Safety, E.R. Lachapelle (Colorado Sports, U.S.A. 1970)
Cross Country Skiing, Rob Hunter (Spurbooks U.K. 1977)
Cross Country Skiing Today, J. Caldwell (Stephen Greene Press U.S.A. 1977)
Frostbite, Bradford Washburn (Museum of Science, Boston U.S.A. 1963)
Hypothermia, Theodore C. Lathrop M.D. (Mazamas U.S.A. 1975)
La Grande Traversée de Jura, Bernard Walger (Dept. du Doubs, France 1977)
Modern Snow & Ice Techniques, Bill March (Cicerone Press U.K. 1973)
Mountain & Cave Rescue (Mountain Rescue Committee U.K. 1975)
Movin' On, Harry Roberts (Stone Wall Press U.S.A. 1977)
Nordic Touring and Cross Country Skiing, M. Brady (Dreyer, Norway, 1977)
Outdoor First Aid, Brown & Hunter (Spurbooks U.K. 1977)
Outdoor Living, M.R.A. Tacoma (U.S.A. 1974)
Rock & Mountain Climbing, R. & J. Mendenhall (Stackpole U.S. 1975)
Safety on the Hills, U.K. Scout Association 1973
Ski Nordique, M. Brady (Editions du Jour (Canada) 1972)
Ski the Nor-Way
Ski Touring, Osgood & Hurley (Tuttle, (Japan) 1969)
Survival & Rescue, Brown & Hunter (Concise Books, Canada, 1977)
Walking Softly in the Wilderness, John Hunt (Sierra Club, U.S.A. 1978)
Waxing for Cross Country Skiing, Brady & S.K. Jemstad (Wilderness Press U.S.A.)
Wilderness Skiing, Tejade & Steck (Sierra Club, U.S.A. 1972)
Winter Camping & Hiking, John Danielsen (Adirondack Mountain Club, U.S.A. 1977)

MAGAZINES

The following magazines carry regular XC and Ski Touring features:-

Backpacker Magazine (U.S.A.)
Mariah (U.S.A.)
Nordic World (U.S.A.)
Outdoor Canada (Canada)
Plein Air (France)
Ski Magazine (Gt. Britain)
Ski Survey (Gt. Britain)